An American Travesty

A volume in the series

 Adolescent Development and Legal Policy

EDITED BY FRANKLIN E. ZIMRING

Also in the series:

Double Jeopardy: Adolescent Offenders with Mental Disorders
by Thomas Grisso

An American Travesty

Legal Responses to Adolescent Sexual Offending

Franklin E. Zimring

Foreword by Francis A. Allen

University of Chicago Press | *Chicago & London*

Franklin E. Zimring is the William G. Simon Professor of Law at the University of California, Berkeley School of Law. He is the author of numerous books, including most recently, *The Contradiction of American Capital Punishment*, and the co-editor of *A Century of Juvenile Justice*, the latter published by the University of Chicago Press.

The University of Chicago Press, Chicago 60637
The University of Chicago Press, Ltd., London
© 2004 by The University of Chicago
All rights reserved. Published 2004
Printed in the United States of America
13 12 11 10 09 08 07 06 05 04   1 2 3 4 5

ISBN: 0-226-98357-9 (cloth)

Library of Congress Cataloging-in-Publication Data

Zimring, Franklin E.
    An American travesty : legal responses to adolescent sexual
offending / Franklin E. Zimring.
        p.   cm. — (Adolescent development and legal policy)
    Includes bibliographical references and index.
    ISBN 0-226-98357-9 (cloth : acid-free paper)
    1. Teenage sex offenders—Legal status, laws, etc.—United States.
2. Sex crimes—United States. 3. Juvenile courts—United States.
I. Title. II. Series.

KF9802.Z56 2004
364.15'3'08350973—dc22

                                                    2003017512

Contents

Foreword

Professor Zimring's particular focus in this book is on a small but important area of penal policy—that concerned with the societal response to the juvenile sex offender. Viewed more broadly, however, the book presents a highly sophisticated analysis of the role of verified knowledge in the formation and application of public policy. The problems encountered in defining the relations of knowledge and policy are not new. As early as January 1776, John Adams in a letter to George Wythe complained, "Mankind seems to have an aversion to the science of government." We may be sure that Adams did not have in mind the particular issues that Zimring confronts, but it may be significant that from the very beginning of the Republic perceptive observers understood that the relation of "science" and "government" constituted an important area of disagreement and discord in a democratic society.

At the outset one is confronted by the attitude, not only of the general public, but of legislators, judges, and lawyers, that verified knowledge is irrelevant, or at least not essential, to the formulation of penal policy. This stance, while perhaps not wholly unique to penal justice, is far more apparent there than in most other important areas of public policy. Many of its consequences are clearly apparent. Failing to examine critically the factual predicates of proposed penal measures and maintaining an almost total disinclination toward careful auditing of the actual impact of measures already in place both tend, particularly in periods of great agitation about crime, to a penal policy often based on emotional sloganeering and a plethora of unintended and undiscovered consequences. Thus, as Professor Zimring describes it, a number of states have enacted registration and notification laws intended to apply to certain types of repetitive adult sex offenders. In a fit of absent-mindedness, legislatures have employed statutory language apparently broad enough to encompass offenders in early adolescence, even though the latter group often presents entirely different problems from adult offenders and very different long-term dangers to the community. Thus fourteen-year-old boys who have committed single acts of sexual aggression against younger children may be transformed into lifelong social pariahs, without achieving, in so doing, significant advantage to the community.

It is not difficult to speculate on the reasons for the antipathy of the general public to the uses of organized knowledge in responding to the perceived menace of criminal behavior. It may be said, for example, that in a time when increasing resort to force characterizes the conduct of government in a wide spectrum of activities, it is perhaps not surprising that to many persons the enlarged use of force is the simple and sufficient instrument for the suppression of crime. Perhaps less obvious are the reasons for prevailing attitudes toward the nature and uses of knowledge in the legal community. In recent decades attitudes of lawyers have tended to a deep agnosticism, and sometimes scorn, toward efforts to collect and organize knowledge in the social disciplines. Opinions in the Supreme Court of the United States seem to reveal, even there, attitudes bordering on the cavalier. In short, lawyers, including lawyers serving on courts or in executive and legislative departments, have often failed to evidence wisdom about, or even interest in, the uses and limitations of systematic knowledge in policy making, particularly in the penal area. Legal education must bear substantial responsibility for the situation. This is not to ignore that in a considerable number of law schools important efforts are going forward to collect verifiable knowledge relevant to policymaking and testing. But such efforts play no large part in the education of most law students, and some current intellectual trends in the law schools may exacerbate a dangerous insouciance toward knowledge-based scholarship, both on the part of the faculty and students.

One of the principal conclusions to be derived from Zimring's discussion, however, is that policy making involves more than collection and application of reliable knowledge. In its most fundamental aspects penal policy is an expression of values. Personal, social, and political values are often in conflict; and policy making, therefore, is importantly concerned with determining which values are to be given priority and how they are to be expressed. If, as sometimes seems to be the case, the democratic majority today favors the values of extreme retribution for criminal behavior and stringent incapacitation of offenders almost to the exclusion of any modifying considerations, then convincing knowledge that such draconian policies damage competing values may have only small relevance for policy.

Yet the realms of knowledge and values ought not to be thought of as rigorously separated. What we believe ought to be is profoundly affected by what we believe reality to be. The converse may also be true: the "ought" may significantly determine our conception of the "is." In many instances, therefore, policy represents an interaction between values and knowledge. Increased knowledge, if attended to, may modify values, or at least modify the means of their expression. Much legislation affecting juveniles in recent years can be convincingly shown to be of dubious social advantage. Some measures, by failing to take into account the immaturity and inexperience of child and adolescent offenders, violate the principle of blameworthiness in dispensing penal sanctions: punishments should not exceed the deserts of the offender, and the immaturity of the adolescent is an essential factor in that calculation. Other measures, as Professor Zimring shows, impose strong incapacitative sanctions on groups of adolescents, the large majority of whom pose no threat to the community after the initial unlawful assault. One effect of measures such as these is the return to the community of a group of persons in their late twenties or early thirties already behind their contemporaries in establishing stable family and employment relations, handicaps that they may never overcome. The existence of such persons in the community represents not only personal tragedies but also makes no contribution to the safety and security of the population.

It may be that there are members of the community so committed to the values underlying harsh retribution and incapacitation of offenders that, even with full knowledge of the consequences of the recent penal measures directed to juveniles, they would continue to support the recent legislation. It seems likely, however, that much of its support comes from persons uninformed about either the provisions or the social costs of these measures. The presence of the latter group gives rise to formidable challenges: those of acquiring a fuller store of verifiable knowledge relevant to these issues and of effective communication of the knowledge to policymakers and the public at large. There are large areas where such crucial knowledge does not exist. Acquiring it will require greater commitment of efforts and funds. The prospects of effectively communicating the new knowledge to policymakers and the public, given current political realities, are of course discouraging. Perhaps greater attention to strategies of persuasion is needed. Yet even under present conditions the purveyors of verifiable knowledge have won occasional small victories, and we may hope for more. Professor Zimring here provides an important step along the way.

Francis A. Allen

Acknowledgments

The debts accumulated in the production of this volume are more numerous and more diverse than those that small books usually incur. First there is the inspiration for an entire monograph series on adolescent development and justice system policy, of which this book is the second installment, provided by the superb series of monographs produced many years ago by the National Institute of Mental Health under the leadership of Saleem Shah. That Crime and Delinquency series showed how modest investments could bring a unified structure and approach to understanding topics of interest to scholars and policy analysts. The Research Network on Juvenile Justice of the John D. and Catharine T. MacArthur Foundation provided both financial support and the guidance of an editorial board whose members include Laurence Steinberg, Elizabeth Scott, Thomas Grisso, Jeffrey Fagan, Edward Mulvey, and Michael Wald. Laurie Garduque, a member of both the foundation and the research network, rescued the monograph series from early administrative problems that threatened its launch. Lynn Boyter, Marnia Davis, Karen Chin, and administrative staff at Temple and the University of California, Berkeley worked hard to make the monograph series a reality.

A volume on adolescent sexual offenders was an obvious priority in the series for the same reason that the effort was difficult to staff and to launch. No scholar of American juvenile justice was expert on sexual offending and its treatment. No scholarly literature on the topic had been produced by experts on legal institutions, criminology, or juvenile justice. I needed guidance through the literature on juvenile sex offenders and sex offenses and was lucky to get the help of Sue Righthand, a treatment professional in the field who had surveyed and organized the literature on juvenile offending for the Office of Juvenile Justice and Delinquency Prevention in 2000. Dr. Righthand provided help at every turn, with literature references, critical reviews of chapters of the monograph, and suggestions for other readers.

Three Berkeley graduate students served as primary research assistants on this project: Elizabeth Garfinkle, Chrysanthi Leon, and Shanna Connor. Each did important work and left distinctive fingerprints on the research and analysis in the text.

The analysis of the FBI Supplemental Homicide Reports in chapters 2 and 3 would not have been possible without the generous help of two colleagues. James Allen Fox of Northeastern University launched the effort and provided computer runs that made the time series report in chapter 2 feasible. Jeffrey Fagan of Columbia University and the Research Network on Juvenile Justice provided the detailed analysis of juvenile cases reported in chapter 3, and also collaborated with me on the age progression curves also found in chapter 3.

Howard Snyder of the National Center for Juvenile Justice in Pittsburgh was an indispensable resource on victim and offender age patterns, on time trends in juvenile court sex cases, on commitments to institutions, and on several other matters. Melissa Sickmund of the National Center helped on institutional trends. The distributions by age and sex of teen sexual experience discussed in chapter 3 were provided by Thao Le of the National Council on Crime and Delinquency.

I have also benefited from reviews of drafts of part or all of this book by Laurence Steinberg, Laurie Garduque, Elizabeth Cauffman, and Elizabeth Scott of the MacArthur Network.

T. David Brent of the University of Chicago Press provided assistance in launching the monograph venture and in publishing this volume. Toni Mendicino of the Earl Warren Legal Institute and American Journal of Comparative Law at the University of California—Berkeley produced the manuscript and most of its figures.

Introduction

The subject of this book is the law's response to sexual misconduct by children and adolescents. The "American travesty" referred to in the book's title is the failure to take the developmental status of young sex offenders into account when making decisions about appropriate legal responses. The clinical, predictive, and moral significance of sexual conduct are significantly influenced by the age and developmental status of the offender. When the legal response to such behavior does not take such matters into account, the results are both unjust and saddening. So one major objective of this book is to provoke developmental specificity in the design of policies toward sexual misconduct.

But the failure of legal policy toward sex offenses to appreciate the offender's developmental status is only one symptom of a larger set of problems that beset the attempt to create rational policy toward sexual misconduct by the young. In the modern politics of criminal justice, policy toward sex offenders is often based on monolithic images of alien pathologies; it is rarely based on facts. The extraordinary heterogeneity of sex offenders and sex offenses is almost never appreciated in the legislative process. Policies are crafted in fearful haste, often as symbolic gestures to honor the crime victims whose suffering has inspired them. The factual foundations for major shifts in policy are often slender; once laws are passed they are rarely evaluated. Even when compared to the spotty performance in other types of criminal justice policy, American policy toward sex offenders is more extreme in its dependence on stereotypes, more resistant to empirical evidence, and less sympathetic to scientific perspectives. Scholarship and evaluation associated with sex offenders and offenses is weaker by far than mainstream empirical criminology.

rarely based on facts

The knowledge base that informs policy toward adolescent offenders is weaker than the available information about adult offending. Assumptions about adolescent sex offenders in current legislation and debates are often based only on the presumed motives and proclivities of nonadolescent offenders. There is very little sound scientific research on sexual misconduct among children and adolescents, and what little that is available is often ignored. Laws have been passed requiring registration and community notification systems for sex offenders without specifically mentioning juvenile offenders or offenses. But such legislation may cover young offenders even if they were far from the thoughts of those drafting the legislation, and even if the adolescent reality is worlds removed from the stereotypes that determine the legal rules. In New Jersey, adult offenders are regarded as more dangerous in the state's sex offender registration scheme if their victims were under the age of thirteen. That seems rational. But then authorities assume that a ten-year-old offender should also be considered more dangerous when *he* was sexually involved with a child under thirteen. This is precisely the kind of equal treatment of dissimilar cases that is both foolish and unjust.

Law and policy analysis concerning young sex offenders, therefore, suffers from a double disadvantage. First, sex crime policy is an area rife with strong prejudice and weak science. Second, the special circumstances of sexual offending in childhood and adolescence have been even less studied than adult offending. Sexual misconduct among children and adolescents is more heterogeneous and more complicated than among adults, and less documented than even the varieties of adult sexual offending.

The goal of this study is to organize existing knowledge about criminal sexual behavior on the part of youths and to discuss the implications of what we currently know for structuring the legal policies that should be pursued. The first part of the book presents a profile of the juvenile sex offender in the United States and the changing legal and treatment environment that the juvenile sex offender confronts. The book's second part, comprising the last three chapters, builds on this overview to analyze the principles and policies that hold promise for rationalizing and reforming the legal response to the young sex offender.

Competing Images

A competition between two sharply different images lies at the heart of the current conflict regarding policy toward the juvenile sex offender. The first features an analogy with the adult sexual predator, where policy is based on the assumption that the child molester and the rapist are a breed apart, pathological and permanently dangerous. The second image of the juvenile sex offender is essentially similar to young offenders that commit other types of juvenile crime. High rates of crime commission are regrettable hazards of modern adolescence, but the responses of most juvenile courts to this are designed to facilitate the offender's normal transition to adulthood. A fundamental tenant of American juvenile courts is that growing up is a proven cure for crime.

Which of these images is best supported by the facts concerning most juvenile sex offenders? How can we find the appropriate legal responses to juvenile sexual misconduct? These are questions of pressing importance at the start of American juvenile justice's second century.

Part 1

The Juvenile Sex Offender

Chapter 1

Three Case Studies

This chapter presents three case studies illustrating the extraordinary recent history of legal responses to problematic sexual activities of children and teens in the United States. They are meant to provide an introduction to that part of our legal system concerned with child and adolescent sexual misconduct and to some troublesome trends in legal policy.

The Case of the Pediatric Pedophile

The public record is not clear on just what happened at J.G.'s house on September 13, 1995 (and we do not know his full name because of the nondisclosure policy of New Jersey's juvenile courts). J.G.'s sister evidently discovered him that afternoon with most of his clothes off in close contact with an eight-year-old female cousin and his five-year-old sister. Adults were informed and police were notified. J.G. was ten at the time.

A delinquency petition was filed against J.G., charging him "on two counts with conduct that if committed by an adult would constitute first-degree aggravated sexual assault based on the commission of acts of sexual penetration with two victims under the age of thirteen" (*In re Registrant J.G.*, 777 A.2d 891, 892 (N.J. 2001). The charges involving his five-year-old sister were later dropped, but J.G. agreed to plead guilty in juvenile court to a single charge of the "second-degree sexual assault" of his cousin. This offense requires sexual penetration through "the use of force or coercion but the victim does not sustain severe personal injury."

The negotiated agreement that led to J.G.'s plea involved no imposition of pretrial detention or posttrial secure confinement. Instead, as the highest court of New Jersey told the story, "the state recommended the imposition of a suspended sentence subject to two conditions: first, that J.G. continue attendance and treatment at a counseling program known as Family Growth; and, second, that he not be permitted to babysit for or be left alone with any young children" (*In re Registrant J. G.*, 777 A.2d at 894).

Two inferences seem justified by the modest controls and the absence of any punishment in the state's offer to this defendant, who was eleven years old at sentencing. First, the prosecutor did not regard J.G.'s conduct as indicating that he was either currently dangerous or particularly culpable. Second, the incentives for J.G.'s family to accept this offer were quite substantial. The only current conditions proposed for the defendant were therapeutic and preventative. The state in effect made J.G. an offer he couldn't refuse. So the plea agreement was accepted, the suspended sentence was entered, and J.G. continued to receive treatment at the Family Growth program with apparent success.

But sixteen months after the sentence was entered, "the Mercer County Prosecutor served J.G. with notice that, pursuant to Megan's Law, he had been classified in tier two as a moderate risk [sex] offender, with a registrant risk assessment scale (RRAS) score of 55" (*In re Registrant J. G.*, 777 A.2d at 896). Under New Jersey's Megan's Law, tier two offenders are the subjects of special notices to schools and day-care centers in the neighborhoods where they reside so that protective measures might be taken to offset the sexual dangers they are thought to pose.

The risk score of this boy, now twelve-and-a-half years old, had been computed by adding up all the factors that would make the conduct that J.G. admitted to committing at age ten into a very serious crime if an adult had done it—the penile penetration of an eight-year-old girl. The district attorney wished to notify the day-care centers and schools of the area where J.G. lived to protect themselves against him.

J.G.'s legal counsel objected to the factual basis for such a high Megan's Law score for a twelve-year-old boy who had been ten when the offense took place. His lawyer offered evidence that the vaginal penetration his client had acknowledged in his juvenile court plea had never in fact taken place. In sworn testimony, the chief therapist of J.G.'s court-ordered counseling testified that

> although J.G. had admitted in his plea to an act of penetration, she did not believe he understood the meaning of the word. She testified that J.G. equated rape with sex, and that he understood sex to mean the act of "rubbing against someone." She testified that his limited ability to speak English impaired his ability to communicate accu-

rately. She also testified that J.G., through the use of anatomically correct dolls, had told her that when the incidents occurred involving alleged sexual assaults of his cousin and his sister during which he laid down on top of each of them, all of them were wearing underwear. . . . "Mrs. Paugalos [the therapist] testified that in her opinion J.G. had not penetrated either his cousin or his sister on the occasion in question. She based her opinion on the September 18, 1995 medical examination of J.G.'s sister that had resulted in an intact hymen and "no signs of sexual abuse" as well as on her experience and extensive opportunities to interview and interrogate J.G. about those incidents and related matters during the past 45 months. On cross-examination, Mrs. Paugalos was questioned about a statement to the police made by J.G.'s older sister to the effect that when she entered the room (on September 13, 1995) J.G.'s cousin was unclothed and J.G. was on top of her with his penis exposed out of his underwear. Mrs. Paugalos responded that based on her impressions, J.G.'s version of the event was more reliable because he displayed to her no intent or desire to minimize the extent of his . . . responsibility for what had occurred. (*In re Registrant J.G.,* 777 A.2d at 898)

For those puzzled about why the location of a ten-year-old's penis should receive so much attention by the highest court of New Jersey five years after the incident, a brief summary of that state's Megan's Law will provide a necessary background. Megan's Laws are named after Megan Kanka, a New Jersey child who was seven years old when raped and killed by an adult neighbor who had previously been imprisoned for sexual predation against child victims. The strategy that sets the Megan's Laws of the 1990s apart from some earlier state laws that required sex offenders to register with police authorities is the use of public notification rather than registration with law enforcement. The central goal is to notify residents of those persons in their neighborhood who may pose a threat to commit sex crimes, thereby encouraging the private citizens to take precautions against such persons.

Some form of Megan's Law is now a universal element of criminal justice in all fifty states. The New Jersey version of Megan's Law divides sex offenders into three classifications. The least-serious class of offender—Class 1—need only register with local law enforcement. A Class 2 offender, however, becomes the subject of formal notification to all elementary, middle, and high schools within a two-mile radius of his residence. Class 3 offenders receive more extensive public notice.

In the mid-1990s, New Jersey law evidently provided that persons convicted of sex offenses in juvenile court are fully covered by that state's Megan's Law, and the system that had evolved provided that juvenile conduct should be classified by the same criteria and scores as adult conduct. Under that scoring system, J.G. was catapulted into a Class 2 offender status for his admitted conduct on September 13, 1995 because (a) his victim was under thirteen and (b) his admitted penetration of his cousin added fifteen more points, which pushed him up to a score of 42. Without the penetration, J.G.'s conduct would have only totaled a score of 27, in which case the neighborhood schools would not be contacted. So the capacity and conduct of J.G. at age ten was suddenly of central importance some years later because New Jersey judged the sexual behavior of children and adults by identical standards.

But was ten-year-old J.G. what New Jersey residents were really worried about when they made sexual contact with children a form of sex crime that warranted special precautions in the community? Should J.G. be regarded as a pedophile at age ten because his only sexual contacts are with young children? What if his partner had been twelve years old when he was ten? Should he still be regarded as especially dangerous because she was under thirteen? Would the twelve-year-old girl be regarded as specially dangerous if she were prosecuted because of J.G.'s tender years? And should the sexual conduct of ten-year-old boys with eight-year-old girls be judged by the same standards as the sexual behavior of twenty-eight-year-old men with eight-year-old girls?

The legal policy implications of classifying J.G.'s actions as if they were those of an adult are worth preliminary mention. Juvenile courts regard children and youth as unfinished and changeable personalities—that is to say, as works in progress. Megan's Laws assume sexual conduct is evidence of fixed and deviant proclivities. Which assumption better suits the reality of the sexual behavior of ten-, twelve-, and fourteen-year-olds? If J.G. is to be regarded as a sex offender for his acts with his cousin, what about his cousin's conduct?

Why doesn't a child protective law like Megan's Law treat the behavior of young children differently than that of adults? Is J.G.'s behavior at age ten a strong predictor of future sexual dangerousness? If so, why did the New Jersey juvenile court allow him to continue living in the community with no special restraint other than a ban on babysitting young children? If not, why does state legislation stigmatize and render permanent the status of sex offender that was so informally conferred without serious factfinding on a ten-year-old boy?

The legal problems of J.G. also push us to ask a series of questions from a behavioral science perspective that test the rationality of policies in New Jersey. What does behavioral science know about the clinical and predictive significance of sexual conduct like J.G.'s at age ten? Is such behavior abnormal from either a developmental or a statistical perspective? Does J.G.'s behavior at ten predict particular problems with his sexual citizenship as an adult? If so, what should state authorities do to alter the risks of his future harm? Should such an intervention be considered punishment, or treatment, or both? If one were to draft a rational sexual registration and community notification law, would it ever cover persons such as ten-year-old J.G.?

Eight Boys and a Girl in Berkeley

While the saga of J.G. made headlines nationally, the second case study took place in northern California and was picked up only by the local media. It took place in Berkeley, a diverse and sophisticated middle-class community of 120,000 across the bay from the city of San Francisco. The first news coverage of the primary incident was published two weeks after the fact, when the *San Francisco Chronicle* reported:

> Seven male students from a Berkeley middle school have been arrested in a five-hour kidnapping and rape of a 12-year-old girl with learning disabilities. . . . Six of the Willard Middle School students have been suspended pending a continuing investigation of the reported attack that began on campus and moved to nearly a dozen other locations. . . . The students appeared to have gained the trust of a girl "who doesn't have the same kind of emotional and intellectual filters that a student that age might ordinarily have," said Berkeley school district spokeswoman Karen Sorlo. Police Lieutenant Russ Lopes said the girl, a student at the [middle] school who has a mental capacity of a third grader, was first attacked somewhere on campus and later at 11 places near school grounds, including a shed and bushes. The alleged attackers who were arrested in the days after the alleged rape and have be released to their parents, could face charges of kidnapping, oral copulation, and rape once the case was forwarded to the . . . district attorney's office." (*San Francisco Chronicle*, November 9, 2000, p. A27.)

The next phase of the case to receive media attention was the formal charging one week later when three of the seven boys were charged with

"oral copulation and false imprisonment as well as misdemeanor battery."
While all the boys had been released to the custody of their parents after
the earlier police arrests, the three who had been formally charged were
then detained in juvenile court. No charges of rape, or kidnapping, or any
forcible sexual conduct were filed against the two thirteen-year-old and
one fourteen-year-old defendants who were formally charged. And no effort was made to transfer any of the cases from juvenile to criminal court.
The three boys who had been charged and detained were called by the
investigating police officer "the most serious offenders," although all of the
boys originally under investigation had illegal sexual contact with the victim. The story did not reveal what aspects of their conduct were supposed
to have made the three detained boys more culpable than the other four
participants.

The final chapter in the published record of this case study hit the news-
stands on November 17, 2000, the day after the story reporting the charging decision and three weeks after the original incident. The *San Francisco
Chronicle* again: "A 12-year-old Berkeley girl who was sexually assaulted by
classmates last month was attacked last week at another Berkeley school
where she had been transferred after the first assault. . . . The girl was
moved to Martin Luther King, Jr. Middle School after last month's reported attack, school officials said. They acknowledged that the girl, who
has learning disabilities, received no special protection."

This new incident was described in starkly different ways by police and
school officials. "The girl was conned into going with a young man into
a secluded area that she was unfamiliar with—she's not a regular student
there of course—and she was raped by him," was the police account. "In a
letter sent to parents," the school principal "described the incident as 'two
students engaged in sexual activity in the bushes during lunchtime.'" The
boy was thirteen years old.

However this second incident might be described, its implication for
the educational future of the twelve-year-old girl was quickly realized. "After the second attack, police and school officials met and decided the girl
must either be schooled at home or attend school with constant supervision
from an aide or some type of guard. . . . She is not attending King [Middle
School]. . . . Teachers are meeting to design a sex education lesson plan for
the next few days that include a live performance of 'Nightmare on Puberty
Street,' a play dealing with issues of peer pressure, abstinence and parent-
teen communication" (*San Francisco Chronicle*, November 17, 2000).

Even without a richer and more carefully constructed account of the
facts of this tragedy, an astonishing variety of difficult and important ques-

tions are raised by the newspaper's reporting of these events. The twelve-year-old girl in these episodes was sexually exploited, humiliated, and eventually driven from two public middle schools as a result of the conduct of eight boys. The way that word gets around about sex in middle schools, it is unlikely that she will ever again be a student in any Berkeley middle school in the educational mainstream. Her compliance in any of the acts of sexual misconduct is in no sense relevant to the harm she suffered. Her status as a severely damaged victim is beyond question.

But how should we describe and respond to the assortment of eight different thirteen-, fourteen-, and fifteen-year-old boys who participated in this catastrophe? The descriptions of the boys' behavior in the local paper range from serious crimes such as kidnapping and rape (where the law might disregard the girl's compliance because of her age, her handicap, and the deception by some of the boys) to sexual misconduct that deserves no more than school discipline and disapproval ("two students engaged in sexual activity in the bushes during lunchtime").

There would be no such ambiguity if an adult had "conned" this twelve-year-old victim into even the most compliant sexual relations. What is there in the predatory behavior of these eight boys that makes unqualified blameworthiness harder to assign? To be sure, the offenders are immature, but how should their youth influence judgments about culpability? And why don't the police urge criminal prosecution of all the boys who shared in the sexual abuse of an obviously disadvantaged girl subjected to a marathon of sexual humiliation? Why not felony child abuse changes of the kind that any adult predator would certainly face? Why not incarceration?

The Willard Middle School in Berkeley is not in a bad neighborhood. Where were the other students the afternoon of the first attack, the good kids we would expect to refuse to participate in the humiliation and instead protest the abuse? Are all the boys at Willard monsters? Are all the seven participants? One twelve-year-old witness who neither reported the episode nor protested the exploitation told his father, "Daddy, I was scared. I didn't want the other kids to think I was a punk." How many of the seven boys who participated in that first marathon of abuse also felt coerced by peer pressure not to be a coward, and also were afraid that nonparticipation would be taken as a public admission of their sexual inadequacy? It is possible that a mix of coercion and the fear of losing status generated pressures on some of the seven boys in the initial episode that were not unlike the pressures that produced the victim's continued compliance. Perhaps there were a number of victims of the events of October 25, 2000, though none of the boys was anywhere near as damaged by those events as the girl.

Are there questions of actuarial risk that we should ask when trying to make sense of the legal accountability and appropriate sanctions for the seven young boys in the first Berkeley attack? What risk of future sexual crimes does each of the boys represent if not removed from the community? If any of them are to be considered rapists in this incident, are they likely to sexually re-offend? Are any of these seven at high risk of future *forcible* sexual conduct? Of sex abuse five and ten years in the future with another twelve-year-old girl? Of future exploitive or coercive efforts to seduce peers of the opposite sex?

If only the last set of risks are obviously linked in the initial involvement with the girl, how important should a juvenile or criminal court regard a teen male's willingness to misrepresent facts and emotions when trying to persuade age peers to consent to sex? Should boys who misrepresent their feelings or facts in an effort to get teenage girls to participate in sex be regarded as sex criminals?

It is important to ask about the extent to which information concerning adult males who sexually abuse twelve-year-old girls provides us with guidance on the types of risks posed by these eight boys in their early teens. Is information on adult males who forcibly rape older girls and women relevant to judgments about the future conduct of these boys? Or is the appropriate comparison group that of adult men who lie and manipulate age peers to obtain consent to sex? Or, more broadly, *is* there a comparison group of adult males that is at all useful for determining the current culpability and future prospects of these eight boys in Berkeley?

And what of that thirteen year old, acting alone, who sought out the young girl now famous in local eighth-grade circles for her conduct at Willard School and talked her into a public act of sexual involvement during lunch break in the community's only other middle school—the place that was her last, best hope for mainstream public schooling? That single but highly visible act may have been the most harmful for the victim. There was no obvious peer pressure involved, although the boy's principal motive clearly was showing off.

Is this predatory thirteen-year-old boy the moral equivalent of a forcible rapist for taking public advantage of a girl who was notoriously compliant and well below grade level? If the content of his character is well below the minimum a community expects of its members, should the juvenile court subject him to a program of sexual and moral education? If the state were to assume the responsibility for teaching youths courses in sexual ethics, should these tutorials be offered through the schools ("Nightmare on Puberty Street"), the courts, or in social service agencies? Should they be taught to wayward youths only or to all boys?

Finally, the reported accounts of the two incidents indicate that all eight boys penetrated the mouth or genitals of a child under thirteen. Were this New Jersey, should they all be considered Class 2 sexual menaces? Should we draft laws to ensure this result?

How Not to Draft a Statute

Like other states in recent years, Idaho passed legislation in 1998 establishing the Sexual Offender Registration, Notification, and Community Right-to-Know Act. The first section of this statute contains a set of legislative findings that rehearses the factual assumptions that are the premises on which the regulatory scheme is based. The Idaho offender registration findings assert that sexual offenders present a significant risk of re-offending and that providing public access to information about such offenders assists parents in the protection of their children. The 173-word findings for Idaho Code § 18-8302 are reproduced as the left-hand column of box 1.

Idaho also passed a companion statute entitled the Juvenile Sex Offender Registration Notification and Community Right-to-Know Act, Idaho Code § 18-8402, and provided a set of findings for this juvenile version (reproduced as the right-hand column of box 1). The legislative findings for the juvenile legislation are 180 words in length, all but 7 of which repeat the 173 words that constitute the findings for the adult Sexual Offender Act in § 8302 of Title 18. The additional language is the insertion of the word "juvenile" on four separate occasions before the term "sex offenders" and the addition of the phrase "or adjudicated delinquent" after the term "convicted" at the end of the earlier set of finding's lengthy first sentence.

What this text illustrates is a particularly destructive form of legislative plagiarism. The introductions to these two pieces of legislation are identical in every substantive sense, adding to the one on the right only the word "juvenile" with no thought about whether the age, experience, or biology of children and adolescents makes their sexual behavior significantly different from that of adults. Moreover, many of the allegations in the adult findings lack support from research, while the copycat language used in the case of juveniles produce allegations that are more often than not flatly contradicted by research, as we shall learn in chapter 3.

This mindless borrowing of assumptions about adults and applying it to children and adolescents would be irresponsible in any context, but is

Box 1. Idaho's Separate but Equal Adult and Juvenile "Findings" Sections

Idaho Sexual Offender Registration Notification and Community Right-to-Know Act

Idaho Code § 18-8302, *Findings*

The legislature finds that sexual offenders present a significant risk of re-offense and that efforts of law enforcement agencies to protect their communities, conduct investigations and quickly apprehend offenders who commit sexual offenses are impaired by the lack of current information available about individuals who have been convicted of sexual offense who live within their jurisdiction. The legislature further finds that providing public access to certain information about convicted sexual offenders assists parents in the protection of their children. Such access further provides a means for organizations that work with youth or other vulnerable populations to prevent sexual offenders from threatening those served by the organizations. Finally, public access assists the public to be observant of convicted sex offenders in order to prevent the offenders form recommitting sex crimes. Therefore, this state's policy is to assist efforts of local law enforcement agencies to protect communities by requiring sex offenders to register with local law enforcement agencies and to make certain information about sex offenders available to the public as provided in this chapter.

Idaho Juvenile Sexual Offender Registration Notification and Community Right-to-Know Act

Idaho Code § 18-8402, *Findings*

The legislature finds that juvenile sex offenders present a significant risk of re-offense and that efforts of law enforcement agencies to protect their communities, conduct investigations and quickly apprehend offenders who commit sex offenses are impaired by the lack of current information available about individuals who have been convicted or adjudicated delinquent of sex offenses who live within their jurisdiction. The legislature further finds that providing public access to certain information about convicted sexual offenders assists parents in the protection of their children. Such access further provides a means for organizations that work with youth or other vulnerable populations to prevent juvenile sexual offenders from threatening those served by the organizations. Finally, public access assists the public to be observant of convicted juvenile sex offenders in order to prevent the offenders from recommitting sex crimes. Therefore, this state's policy is to assist efforts of local law enforcement agencies to protect communities by requiring juvenile sex offenders to register with local law enforcement agencies and to make certain information about juvenile sex offenders available to the public as provided in this chapter.

Source: Idaho Penal Code.

particularly problematic when the findings themselves speak of the special needs for protection of children. Idaho, in the guise of child protection, has failed in its obligation to take childhood seriously by assuming that the sexual acts of children are the equivalent to those of adults.

The copycat nature of Idaho's legislation to compel the registration and community notification of juvenile sex offenders does not stop at the legislative findings of fact that are profiled in the box 1. It turns out that the list of offenses that require registration for adults and for youth is also identical. The problem posed by this parallel treatment can be seen in one of the listed crimes, "Lewd Conduct with Minor Child under Sixteen" (§ 18-1508), which provides in part that "[a]ny persons who shall commit any lewd or lascivious act or acts upon or with the body of a minor child . . . shall be imprisoned . . . for a term of not more than life." The prohibited acts include "manual-genital contact . . . done with the intent of arousing the sexual desires . . . of such minor child."

It is clear from this wording that two fifteen-year-old adolescents engaged in consensual manual stimulation of each other's genitals (what in more euphemistic terms used to be called "heavy petting") are both guilty of an Idaho felony that requires them to register as sex offenders until at least age twenty-one. Further, the statutory language might also mean that any fifteen year old caught masturbating has thereby committed a "lewd act . . . upon the body of a minor child." (There is no express requirement in § 18-1508 that victim and offender must be different persons, although I would hope an activist judge might impose an interpersonal requirement on the broad language of the statute. Why Idaho's penal policy would be well served by classifying juvenile masturbation as a felony I do not know. Requiring a victim other than the offender provides an easy escape.)

Even with all these faults, the Idaho approach to juvenile sexual conduct is by no means the nation's worst. The Idaho law allows most juvenile offenders to be removed from its registry at age twenty-one, while many other states make no distinction between adults and youths in registration and community notification.

The three case studies in this chapter are a mixture of the old and the new. The sexual behavior described is in no sense novel—children and youth have been engaged in similar conduct throughout history. One of the ironies of child and adolescent development is that each new phase of sexual development begins shrouded in the same abysmal ignorance that characterized all previous generations. No matter how much we try, modern Western societies do not seem to learn much about sexual conduct that transfers over to future generations at the point of sexual maturation. So each new generation seems as much to invent sex as to inherit knowledge of its practice.

But if the sexual behaviors in this chapter's case studies are all too familiar, the legal reactions to such conduct include many responses that are unprecedented in the legal systems of any developed nation. In the United States at the turn of the twenty-first century, legal policy toward adolescent sexual conduct has been swept up into a restructuring of registration and reporting requirements for adult sex offenders. It is now frequently assumed in legislation and litigation that adolescent and adult sexual behavior should be judged by the same standards of culpability, clinical significance, and indications of future danger to the community. Much of this new trend in policymaking has proceeded with no explicit awareness that the behaviors of children and teens would be subject to the new regimes. And there is no evidence that they should be.

There is also a second series of recent legal changes that have been expressly designed for teenage males and administered by juvenile courts. Rates of referral to juvenile court for sexual offending have not increased substantially since the mid-1980s in the United States, but a new clinical cottage industry has been created to provide treatment for those referred to court for sexual behavior that violates community and legal standards. All of the boys whose cases were heard in juvenile court in the two introductory case studies in this chapter were sent to such sexual-counseling programs, which now number nearly 600 across the nation. What is the content of treatment in such programs? Are they appropriate responses to sex offending? Do they change behavior? What alternatives exist to such programs? Do such programs assume that adolescent needs and behaviors are distinct from those of other offenders or do they simply apply the same programs that are used for adults? When does a juvenile court believe that referral to a counseling program is not a sufficient community response to an act of sexual offending?

This book has three aims. The first is to criticize the assumption that adolescent sexual conduct has the same clinical and predictive significance as the same conduct committed by adults. I show that the assumptions of equivalence that emanate from regulations like those J.G. faced in New Jersey are flatly contradicted by the known facts about adolescent behavior. "One size fits all" assumptions about adolescent and adult sexual conduct in registration, punishment, and notification schemes simultaneously disserve the interests of both youthful offenders and the public safety. In fact, the obvious need to design responses to sexual conduct with close attention to the developmental status of offenders makes a compelling case for the critical importance of a developmental perspective on all adolescent offending. Thus, horror stories about the same-for-all-ages point counting in New Jersey are examples of a broader problem—legal regulations that ignore the uniqueness of childhood and adolescence.

The second aim of this book is to profile the behavioral dimensions of harmful adolescent sexual conduct, and the difficult trade-offs that must be confronted when policies about adolescent sexual offending are constructed. Rejection of adult models of culpability and prognosis is only the first step in the establishment of rational policy in response to sexual offenses on the part of youths. Appreciating the volatility and experimentation that characterize most adolescent sexual misconduct does not in any way mean that the conduct itself is less destructive. The central task of policy toward youth sex crime is minimizing the immediate harms it produces while facilitating the normal maturation of offenders and their victims. What are the harms of adolescent sex offending? Which victims are hurt most, and how might their suffering be diminished? These are questions worth more than one book. But this volume is intended as a small down payment on the larger enterprise of research and analysis that rational policy requires.

The third goal is to produce a policy analysis of specific programs currently used as legal responses to adolescent sex offending. What do we know about the effects of current programs? What do we need to find out? In seeking to answer these questions, I hope to begin constructing an agenda of policy research for this important area of law.

The first part of this book shows the important differences between adult and youthful sexual offenses. Chapter 2 discusses the facts and assumptions about adult sexual offending and offenders in contemporary criminal justice. Chapter 3 presents a discussion of the child and adolescent sex offender. Chapter 4 examines the ideology and practice of juvenile sex-offender treatment.

The second part of the book is an effort at policy analysis. Chapter 5 outlines the strategic aims of American juvenile courts and the extent to which they suggest specific forms of policy toward adolescent sex crime. Chapter 6 provides a framework for reforms in policy toward adolescent sex offenders in American juvenile courts. Chapter 7 discusses registration and notification schemes.

Chapter 2

Continuity and Change in American Sex-Crime Policy

One clear lesson from our review of Idaho's legislation in chapter 1 is that criminal justice policy toward adult sex offenders has a powerful influence on the policies used for younger offenders in both criminal and juvenile courts. For this reason, policy toward adolescent sexual conduct cannot be understood without some exposure to the approach of the criminal justice system to older sex offenders. This chapter provides a brief summary of the criminal law governing sexual conduct and recent trends in its enforcement. In the first part of the chapter I profile the extent of criminal justice involvement in responding to sexual behaviors and the image of the sex offender that animates recent policies. In the second section I review data on recent trends in enforcement and punishment.

Sex Crimes and Offenders

Legal Categories and Theories of Harm

The overlap between sexual conduct and the criminal law is extensive in both theory and practice. If we combine all the offenses in the United States during the year 2000 that were reported to involve some degree of sexual conduct, they would account for at least 200,000 arrests of persons over age eighteen and 15,000 persons under eighteen (U.S. Department of Justice, 2000, p. 226). This aggregate category of all crimes with some sexual element covers a very wide range of degrees of severity and includes at least six different types of presumed criminal harm: (1) force, (2) non-forcible predation, (3) sexual behavior that is unlawful *per se,* (4) public indecency, (5) invasion of the sexual or bodily privacy of a victim, and (6) commercialization of sex. In this section I examine these six categories of sex crimes.

FORCE. The primary criminal law regarding the use of force to generate sexual contact is the crime of forcible rape. Long a serious crime and often a capital offense, rape is defined as engaging in sexual intercourse through the use of force or the threat of force against the victim. Most states have enacted equally serious legislation to prohibit forcing other genital-involved sexual conduct, and these usually cover male victim and same-sex forcible sexual encounters. There are also lesser offenses related to the use of physical force to obtain other forms of sexual contact such as fondling and contact through clothing. The Federal Bureau of Investigation classifies forcible rape as a "Part 1" serious crime and as one of the four Part 1 violent crimes.

ABUSE OF YOUTH. The law prohibits a wide range of predatory sexual contact with persons considered incapable of giving what is deemed legitimate consent to sexual participation. The primary victim categories for these offenses are children of various ages, but other protected groups include the cognitively impaired and the insane, and there are also special prohibitions of sexually aggressive behaviors involving the use of drugs or alcohol to impair the capacity of otherwise competent persons in order to achieve sexual contact. While the sexual use of immature victims was often classified as a "statutory rape" because of the inability of the young to give legal consent, the more appropriate theory of penal liability for this class of sexual conduct is predation without force, in which the wrongfulness of the sexual contact stems from exploitation of the vulnerability and incapacity of the victim.

Figure 2.1 shows the percentage distribution of the fifty states according to the "age of consent"—the earliest age at which a girl's willingness to engage in sexual relations will absolve her partner of criminal liability. Almost all states prohibit sexual intercourse with girls under the age of sixteen and more than one-third restrict consent to seventeen or eighteen year olds.

Whether such predatory liability requires a real gap in the age and capacities of the parties to sexual contact is one major division among states' statutory schemes governing sex with youths. Laws in about half the states do not cover peers in prohibiting sexual contact with older teens, requiring instead an age gap of two, three, four, or five years between the offender's age and that of the victim (see Elstein & Davis, 1997). Others, like Idaho, make no distinction. Frequently, states will have separate offenses for sex with very young children (more severely punished) and for prohibited sex with partners closer to full sexual maturity and the age of consent (e.g., over thirteen).

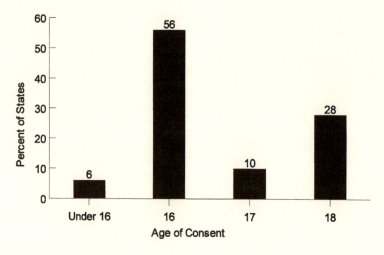

Figure 2.1. Percentage distribution by age of consent to sexual intercourse, fifty states
Source: Elstein & Davis, 1997.

Another set of criminal prohibitions of predatory behavior concerns what are classified as "indecent liberties with a child" or lewd conduct. The range of behaviors prohibited is more extensive than sexual intercourse but, as shown in figure 2.2, the ages of consent making the broader range of conduct criminal are younger.

Thirty percent of the states prohibit "lewd conduct" with a cut-off age under thirteen, fourteen, or fifteen, compared to only 6 percent of the state laws on sexual intercourse. Major states such as Illinois (age thirteen) and California (age fourteen) restrict their prohibition to minors not much older than puberty, while states like Texas (seventeen) and Colorado (eighteen) prohibit the broader range of sexual contacts much later into adolescence and dating. About 40 percent of the states exempt age peers from criminal prohibitions by requiring some age difference between victim and offender before the conduct is forbidden. But three of five age-eighteen states and four of the five age-seventeen states do not exempt age peers from criminal liability.

IMMORAL ACTS. The third category of sex crime mentioned above involves practices that are prohibited *per se*—that is, sexual acts that are criminal regardless of the status or willingness of the parties. A long list of practices were traditionally forbidden, including bestiality, as well as homosexual and heterosexual sodomy (genital/oral and genital/anal contacts). There was also an extensive history of prohibitions against engaging in sexual relations outside of marriage (adultery and fornication). A long

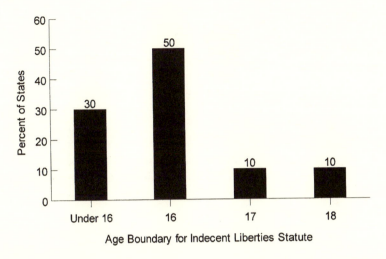

Figure 2.2. Percentage distribution by age of consent to sexual contact, forty-nine states and the District of Columbia
Source: Survey of state laws conducted by Shanna Connor (see appendix A).

trend toward decriminalization of sodomy culminated in 2003 with the U.S. Supreme Court's decision in *Lawrence v. Texas,* 123 S. Ct. 1512 (2003), striking down criminal prohibitions of sodomy between consenting adults (of the same sex) as a violation of the constitutional rights of privacy. A majority of the Court would also find laws prohibiting heterosexual sodomy offensive, while the impact of this case on adultery and fornication prohibitions is unclear.

The theory that justifies *per se* prohibitions of sex between consenting adults is the harm that is assumed to be suffered by the entire community in the face of immoral conduct (or, in the case of adultery, the harm suffered by an innocent spouse and the institution of marriage). The trend toward reform has been based on arguments that the sexual behavior of consenting adults is not a legitimate state concern and that consensual behavior in private does not threaten harm to the community.

PUBLIC INDECENCY. The fourth category of sexual offense is usually called "public indecency," which includes individuals displaying their genitals in public or engaging in publicly visible sexual conduct. Some commercially motivated sexual displays are also prosecuted under public indecency prohibitions (sex clubs and strip shows), but the stereotypical cases of public indecency offenses involve exhibitionists or "flashers," almost always men, who display their sexual organs to strangers. The harm here is the fear or disgust engendered in the involuntary audience of the display—the violation of a person's expectation that walking through one's neighborhood should not involve the risk of being subjected to close contact with another person's sexual organs or behavior. There is also concern that persons willing to publicly display themselves might be high risks for initiating forcible sexual contact, so that the exhibitionist can create fears of both closer contact and force in some members of his audience.

COMMERCIAL PRIVACY. The fifth category of prohibited acts involves the invasions of privacy that result when persons attempt to observe other people in states of undress or nakedness or engaged in sexual activities. This is usually a crime of stealth. The popular term for this kind of offender is "peeping Tom," and the obvious basis of his criminal liability is the distress inflicted on the unwilling subjects of this type of scrutiny. But just as flashers are prosecuted and punished in part because it is feared that they may become rapists, the peeping Tom frightens his victims and the community because it is thought he might also force sexual contact. During an age in which stalking has become a relatively serious crime and social concern, the peeping Tom is easy to regard as a species of stalker.

COMMERCIAL SEX. The sixth distinct category of sex crime has to do with commercial vice involving adults. Almost all developed Western nations now prohibit the commercial exchange of sexual services that are not themselves unlawful. Even when fornication and adultery are not criminally prohibited, sex for money is usually still forbidden. A wide range of sex-for-money behaviors are the subject of criminal prohibition. Prostitution, the act of engaging in sex for hire, has not only been described as "the world's oldest profession" but is the subject of a criminal prohibition of almost equal antiquity. Living off the earnings of prostitutes is often a separate criminal offense. Soliciting a prostitute is also an independent offense in many jurisdictions.

Pornography was until quite recently criminal in most Western nations, and extreme forms of pornography that are considered "obscene" are still prohibited in many states. Child pornography, variously defined, is criminal most everywhere and is currently the subject of concentrated international efforts aimed at its suppression.

The commercial context is regarded as compounding the stigma of behavior that might ordinarily be regarded as merely immoral, and arguments are also made that prostitution is exploitation (and its practitioners victims). So suppressing prostitution is regarded as a way of improving the moral health of the wider community. Also, the money and power associated with the commercialization of sex are often regarded as an opportunity for organized crime.

The Incidence and Prevalence of Sex Crime in the United States

It is not possible to use official statistics to answer such questions as "How much sex crime occurs in the United States?" or "What percentage of the population has ever committed a sex crime?" or "How many active sex offenders are currently at liberty in the United States?" Information on the number of reports by citizens is available for only one offense-forcible rape. Most other offenses are rarely detected (e.g., the peeping Tom) or involve willing participants who would not be likely to bring an offense to the attention of legal authorities (prostitution, much underage sex, and adultery). Even predatory sexual acts with child or other vulnerable victims are rarely reported, so that official statistics are not a good indicator of the prevalence or incidence of these offenses.

There is also good evidence that the number of reported rapes is substantially fewer than the actual total, because victims are embarrassed and afraid and do not inform police. It is a bit ironic that the success of a police agency in developing a trusting relationship with the community often produces an apparent increase in reported rapes because a larger proportion of actual rapes become reported rapes as the reputation of the police improves. Survey data of various kinds do provide some estimates of the incidence and prevalence of several criminal sexual behaviors. Ever since the initial Kinsey Report, it has been known that a substantial proportion of the population commits a wide variety of prohibited sexual acts on a consensual basis (see Kinsey, Pomeroy, & Martin, 1948). Many individuals have engaged in sexual intercourse with persons under the age of consent, patronized prostitutes, or engaged in many other nonforcible practices prohibited by law. But there is little sense in aggregating survey results to generate an estimate of the proportion of the population with some experience of sexual criminality, because any such aggregate number would be meaningless. The vast majority of the sex offenses committed by ordinary citizens produce only trivial to moderate concern for the community. The prototypical sex criminal most feared by the public is violent or preys on children far below the age when they have any sophistication or defenses.

Figure 2.3 provides year 2000 data on police arrests for three classes of sex offenders. The three categories reported in the figure can be seen as a severity scale, going from left to right, in descending order of the seriousness of the charges. Most serious, of course, is the rape category, which includes completed or attempted "carnal knowledge of a female forcible and against her will." While this is only a police charge and may not prove

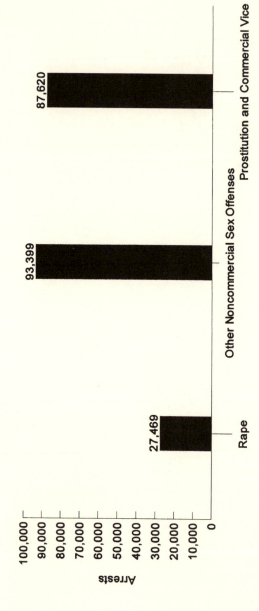

Figure 2.3. Three categories of sex-related arrests in U.S. during 2000
Source: U.S. Department of Justice, 2000.

out at that level of severity, the crime as defined is quite serious, and non-forcible "statutory charges based on age of the female have been excluded" (U.S. Department of Justice, Federal Bureau of Investigation, 2000). At the other end of the severity scale are the more than 80,000 commercial sex cases that are presumably criminal only because of the commercial context. To be sure, acts of physical force and extreme economic coercion are associated with the persons and organizations involved in prostitution and vice, but any charges of robbery or sex by force or abuse of minors lodged against commercial sex practitioners would not be reported in this category. So the commercial sex offenses that fall in this category in figure 2.3 do not involve these aggravating elements. Such charges are clustered at the low end of the seriousness scale for sex offenses, and the sentences handed down in these cases usually reflect that status of low severity.

The middle category in figure 2.3 aggregating a series of "other" sex offenses is extremely heterogeneous. Here are collected an array of charges from public indecency that is just over the lower threshold for police involvement to serious cases of indecent liberties with very young children. Immodest drunks and unlucky teen dates charged with statutory rape are mixed in this category with predatory pedophiles, and there is no account of how most of the over 90,000 arrests in the category break down by seriousness.

The data shows that about 40 percent of all sex arrests are for nonviolent, nonpredatory commercial vice offenses, and that about 15 percent of all persons with sex arrests are charged with rape. The remaining 44 percent of sex arrests, which amount to more than three-fourths of all the arrests for noncommercial sex offenses, are in a category without any clear indication of the seriousness of the offense. The type of audits on samples of this category of arrests that could provide some indication of the distribution of such offenses by seriousness have not been conducted. For this reason, anyone wishing to estimate the rate of arrests in the United States for serious sex crimes cannot rely on published police statistics.

The slightly more than 200,000 arrests for offenses involving sex can seem like a lot or relatively few depending on the standard of comparison. The 27,000 rape arrests are just over 1 percent of the 2.25 million Part 1 arrests recorded in the United States in 2000, approximately double the arrest volume for murder but far fewer than any other of the index offenses. The best standard of comparison for all types of sex offenses is the estimated total of nontraffic offenses in the United States, approximately 14 million in 2000, where sex charges account for 1 arrest in every 70 among those eighteen years and older. To the extent that arrest volume is a good measure of the importance of a category of criminal activity, the sex crimes would appear to be of modest importance. But rape and the sexual abuse of young children are matters of great concern for most citizens, and the volume of arrests is not a good indication of the degree of public worry about the most serious of sex offenses.

More than public anxiety about victimization argues against the use of arrest volume as a meaningful measure of the importance of criminal sexual conduct as a social concern. Arrest volume is a meaningful indicator of the volume of only one of the serious sex crimes-forcible rape, and probably even then only a good indicator of the incidence of forcible rape involving an unacquainted victim and offender. The great majority of serious sexual abuses of children and other dependent populations never come to the attention of police or other public authorities.

Sex Offenses as Lethal Violence

The worst case outcome from a sexual offense is an attack resulting in the victim's death. Since 1976, the Uniform Crime Reports produced by the Federal Bureau of Investigation has reported details about the precipitating circumstances of homicides for cases that lead to arrests. Not all police agencies produce usable data on homicide arrests for all years, but the Uniform Crime Reports keep track of homicide arrests associated with two categories of sex offense: "forcible rape" and "other sex offense." Figure 2.4 reports the annual total of homicide arrests for sex-crime-related killings. There are no corrections in the figure for changing U.S. population or for the population of reporting police agencies in any given year. So the trends over time are not in any sense precise.

During the first decade for which the Uniform Crime Reports collected data on sex-offense homicides, the number of arrests rose from 302 in 1976 to just over 350 in 1979 and 1980, and then fell to 248 by 1984. The increase in the late 1970s and the decrease in the 1980s both parallel trends in total homicide, which peaked in 1980 and fell by about one-third in the earlier years of the 1980s (U.S. Department of Justice, 1976–1984). After 1986, however, the rate of sex-offense killings entered a sustained period of decline, which did not match general homicide trends. While the overall homicide rate increased in the late 1980s, the volume of sex offense killings dropped by half between 1986 and 1994 and continued its drop by half again between 1994 and 1999. In the twenty years after 1980, the volume of sex-offense killings reported in the United States dropped by 80 percent. During these two decades, there were no large drops in reported sex

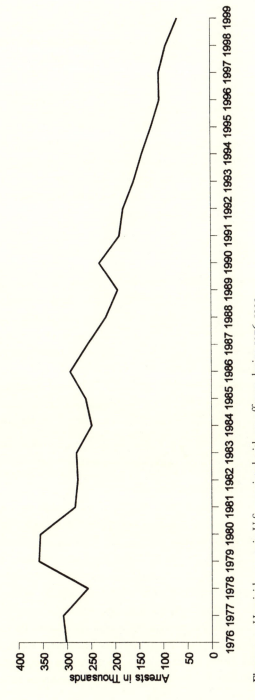

Figure 2.4. Homicide arrests in U.S. associated with sex offenses during 1976–1999
Source: U.S. Department of Justice, supplemental homicide data set, 1975–2000.

offenses and the overall homicide rate had strong up cycles as well as a large downward trend from 1992 to 2000.

The magnitude of the drop in official sex-crime homicide charges makes me suspect that police criteria for classifying killings as sex-crime related may have changed over time, perhaps becoming more conservative by requiring more evidence of a sex-crime circumstance. By 1998 and 1999, the two-year total of 160 sex-crime-related killings were about one-half of 1 percent of total homicide arrests in the United States. The largest category of felony killings, those taking place during the commission of robberies, is more than an order of magnitude greater in its annual death toll.

There is reason for skepticism that the decline by four-fifths in the reported death toll from sexual assaults really represents an 80 percent drop in the risk of sex-crime victims being killed, but the steady decline over two decades and the consistently small numbers in the late 1990s do suggest that the death rate from sex offenses has been falling. So the news about sex-crime killings is good, but any precision in estimating trends over time must wait for more careful analysis of police reporting.

The Contemporary Image of the Sex Offender

The offenses that cause most public concern and motivate special attention to "sex criminals" are crimes of sexual force and predatory abuse of children and youth who lack the capacity to judge the intentions of others or to defend themselves from the sexual aggression of exploitative adults. The image of the rapist and child molester have inspired a series of legal changes in the 1980s and 1990s, including shifts in criminal penalties and the will to impose them, legislation to supplement criminal penalties with extended terms of "civil" commitment to protect communities from the risk of re-offending on release, and the registration and community notification systems that are usually described as "Megan's Laws" (see chapter 1).

The rapist and child molester historically have been sources of public outrage and fear throughout Western nations, and the penalties for cases involving extremely violent rape or molestation have usually been quite severe. The child molester, for example, is so detested among prisoners that he is at high risk of attack by them and often must be held in protective segregation from the general prison population, sometimes in separate facilities (Man & Cronan, 2001/2002; Office of the Inspector of Custodial Services, 2003, p. 42).

A BREED APART? The sexual predator has always occupied a special place in both the popular and, to some extent, the professional understanding of crime and crime policy. While many criminal offenders are regarded as the products of the social conditions in which they are born and grow up, the rapist and the child molester are not believed to be a social type in this sense. Indeed, while it is currently unfashionable to regard most criminal conduct as the product of psychological pathology, the serious sexual offender is an exception to this perception. Thus, while sociologists and other social scientists are regarded as experts about most types of criminal behavior, it is the psychologist of the abnormal who is consulted when sexual predation is the concern.

There are four critical assumptions about sexual offenders that seem to underlie a wide range of recently enacted laws and policies. Together, these assumptions project the image of the sex offender in terms of (1) pathological sexual orientation, (2) sexual specialization, (3) fixed sexual proclivities, and (4) a high level of future sexual dangerousness.

The assumption that sex crimes are produced by sexual pathologies is most clearly reflected in two generations of state laws providing supplemental incapacitation as a "civil" commitment for specially identified "sexually dangerous persons" after they complete prison terms for sex offenses. An early-twentieth-century collection of such laws required a diagnosis of a mental disorder manifest by the commission of sex crimes and permitted secure confinement under civil rather than criminal authority. A later set of such laws was passed in the 1980s and 1990s and upheld against constitutional attack by the U.S. Supreme Court in *Kansas v. Hendricks,* 521 U.S. 346 (1997) (Mass. Gen. Laws Ann. ch. 123A, § 9; Kan. Stat. Ann. § 59-29aO1 (1997); Minn. Stat. § 253B.02 (1997)).

The earlier laws regarding civil commitment for sexually dangerous persons were the product of an era when psychological explanations for a wide variety of criminal and delinquent acts were common. So the clinical psychologizing that underlay the policy toward sex offenders was in no sense unique. But the *Kansas v. Hendricks* generation of civil commitment statutes put state legislatures on record as advocating a pathology theory of serious sex crime offenders when clinical explanations for most other offenses were disfavored.

It is true that special "sexually dangerous person" laws apply only to a subclass of sexual offenders, and that these provisions have been invoked in a very small number of cases. But the assumption of pathology that is reflected in these laws seems also to be the underlying presumption for how the public understands most persons convicted of forcible rape, child molestation of young children, and adults who commit aggravated incest. The standard public assumption is that such conduct is motivated by a clinically significant sexual pathology.

The extent to which this assumption is true is not well documented. Certainly some categories of sex offense are better explained than others by attributing pathological conditions to those who commit them. But a straightforward assessment of the presence or absence of clinically significant abnormalities in large samples of adult subjects arrested for various classes of sex crime is not available.

A second assumption about sex offenders that distinguishes them from other offenders and informs recent legislation and policymaking has to do with their *specialization* in sex offenses. Most repeat criminals are generalists whose criminal histories comprise a variety of different types of offense. Criminal careers are noteworthy for their diversity (Blumstein et al., 1986). Last year's burglary suspect may well be arrested this month for serious assault or robbery. But the stereotypical sex offender that animated policy in the 1990s was not regarded as part of a subculture of general criminality, and fears of recidivism on the part of sex offenders have to do with the likelihood that they will commit further sexual offenses. Special public sex offender notification laws are not enacted in order for citizens to defend themselves against larceny or carjacking.

The third assumption that I believe is made about sex criminality among adults is that the victims selected by sex criminals are a reflection of fixed offender preferences. It is believed that the victim's gender and age and the setting in which the sexual offense takes place reflect the conditions that stimulate the offender, and that any future offenses will likely involve similar targets and settings. The plausibility of this assumption of fixed preferences depends in part on the extent to which the criminal sexual act can be shown to have been produced by a sexual pathology that is manifest in fixed preferences. Yet it is also true that normal human sexuality involves fixed sexual preferences as well. Persons without any clearly abnormal sexual proclivities are likely to still express preferences as to the gender, race, physical features, and age of their partners.

The predominant image of the serious sex offender is of a person with fixed and pathological sexual preferences. If last year's arrest was for conduct involving a seven-year-old female, the offender is presumed to be a pedophile who is likely to seek out further victims of similar age and gender. In the image animating current public policy, these fixed preferences are part of the hardwiring of a sex offender, not apt to change even over long periods of time.

The fourth characteristic of the stereotypical sex offender is that of high dangerousness, with serious recidivism said to be all but inevitable in much of the public discourse on offender registration and community notification. In one of President Clinton's weekly radio addresses, he claimed, "Nothing is more threatening to our families and communities and more destructive of our basic values than sex offenders who victimize children and families. Study after study tell us that they often repeat the same crimes. That's why we have to stop sex offenders before they commit their next crime, to make our children safe and give their parents piece of mind" (www.cnn.com /allpolitics /1996 /news /9608 /24 /clinton.radio /transcript. shtml). In a letter to Assemblyman Dean Andal, former California governor Pete Wilson stated, "In the case of sex offenders—namely rapists and child molesters—the first offense should be the last: they should be locked up for life" (December 9, 1993, www.thevop.com/dean_andal.html). The two elements that produce this distinctive aura of high dangerousness are the seriousness of the expected repeat offense and the very high likelihood it will happen. Despite the notion that sexual targets and pathologies are fixed, the public also fears that last month's peeping Tom or exhibitionist is next month's rapist or child murderer. For this reason, it is not clear what impact studies that find significantly lower than expected recidivism rates would have on public attitudes if the nature of the future offense is expected to be so grave. It is probable that even a 20–25 percent risk of the most serious of sex crimes would be regarded by many persons as posing a great threat.

IMAGE AND REALITY. Several points should be noted about the four assumptions concerning sex offenders just outlined. First, the empirical support for these beliefs is uneven. The sex pathology label fits well for some types of repetitive sexual offending but not with others. Some peeping Toms, many flashers, and many if not most of repetitive child sex abusers have distinct clinical conditions. By contrast, most rapists, and many offenders involved in the opportunistic sexual abuse of children or the incapacitated, do not. When serious sex offenders are compared with those who commit theft or violent crimes, the prevalence of a distinct pathology is greater among sex offenders, but there is nevertheless substantial heterogeneity in almost every category of severe sex crime. And many distinct clinical pathologies—fetishes, for one—do not produce any strong tendencies toward sexual predation.

Figure 2.5 illustrates the overlap between clinically significant diagnoses of sexual pathologies (paraphilia) and noncommercial sex offenses. The overlapping circles show an incomplete relationship between the incidence of sexual pathology and the commission of sex crimes. I suspect that many paraphiliacs do not commit crimes ever or for long periods of time. Indeed, there are several clinical conditions such as fetishes and compulsive cross-dressing disorders in which fulfilling erotic objectives need not violate legal prohibitions. Other paraphiliacs do not act out fantasies that would violate the law. One reason that both the prevalence and incidence of criminality among persons with abnormal sexual preferences is overstated is that the population of persons with paraphiliac preferences of various kinds is not known. How many adults are sexually attracted to children, either exclusively or in addition to others? How many adults have defined fetishes? Assessment studies on populations like college students might provide some good data on the denominator of paraphiliac preference against which the number of criminally active persons could be compared.

Instead of this, current literature begins with samples of persons who have been caught committing sex crimes (Abel 1985). This subsample is not only 100 percent criminal, but is also biased because it overrepresents the most active sexual offenders because they have higher likelihoods of apprehension.

Then there is the very substantial number of sex crimes—including rape and much sexual abuse of minors—that is not committed by persons suffering from clinically diagnosable sexual disorders. What we do *not* know is what percentage of all or even some sexual offenses are the product of paraphilia. With no firm estimate of the incidence of most sex crimes, there is no obviously valid way of making an estimate. Clinical review of the records of a representative sample of persons arrested for a series of offenses might provide an accurate account of the overlap in known cases.

Specialization in the same pattern of offending is also more common among flashers and pedophiles than among burglars and robbers, but forcible rape is one offense committed by persons with a great variety of serious nonsexual offenses in their criminal records. There is also a high degree of variance among offenders in the fixity of sexual preferences, and variation among subgroups in risks of recidivism.

When official criminal records are consulted, there is in fact little evidence that child molesters are more likely than nonsexual offenders to re-offend. When prison release statistics are compared, re-arrest rates are lower one and two years after release for child molesters than for burglars and robbers released from prison. Child molesters released from California

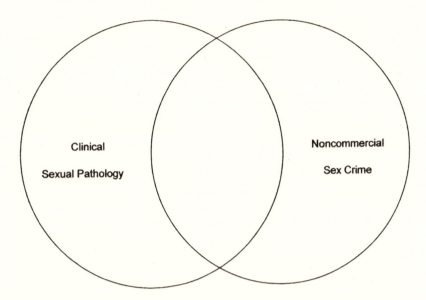

Figure 2.5. Hypothesized overlap between sexual pathologies and noncommercial sex crimes

prisons return within two years at a 27 percent rate, much lower than average for other offense categories (Zimring, 1997). Whether this is evidence that re-offending prevalence is also modest is hotly disputed in the literature. It is argued that low detection rates and the skills of avoiding arrest that experienced offenders acquire over time make the true recidivism rate higher than the official re-arrest rate. There is a dark figure of undetected recidivism that is quite large. But even with statistical manipulations to correct for some downward biases and to provide long-range follow-up, the known recidivism approaches 50 percent.

With all these unanswered factual questions concerning the true profile of sex offenders, the four assumptions we have explored that are commonly made about them are best regarded as theoretical or hypothetical only.

A second important point about the four presumed characteristics of the serious sex offender that I think are driving current policy is that the postulated behavioral patterns of sex offenders are closely related to each other rather than independent. The predominant theory behind sex-crime legislation is that offenders have patterns of specialization and fixed sexual preferences because they are under the influence of a clinically significant sexual pathology that is the continuing force driving the offender's impulses and decisions. The four assumptions are a collective portrait of the pathology-driven behavior believed to characterize the serious sex offender.

The third point that must be made about this set of assumed characteristics is that they seem to have had a very strong influence on the strategies of control that became prevalent in the 1990s. Offender registration, community notification, civil confinement at the end of prison terms, and legal provision for treatments called "chemical castration" (West's Fla. Stat. Ann. § 794.0235, administration of medroproxyprogesterone acetate to persons convicted of sexual battery; West's Cal. Penal Code § 645, medroproxyprogesterone acetate treatment) are all closely linked to a theory of sex crime as the outcome of a fixed, compulsive, and repetitive pathology.

The registration and notification strategies assume that the nature of the future threat posed by an offender can best be determined by reviewing his criminal record. The control strategy only makes sense if the assumptions are true. And the use of sex-specific tools like chemical castration to reduce sexual drive and capacity only promises to prevent one type of criminal recidivism; it is a poor tool for an offender with criminal proclivities that are not specific to sexual conduct.

Changes in Law and Policy

The twenty years after 1980 were a curious mix of undramatic continuity and dynamic change in policy toward sex offenders in the United States.

The fewest changes in legal policy concerned basic prohibitions in the criminal law about sexual conduct. The range of practices prohibited by the criminal law did not change much, and the few changes that have occurred in the past generation have reduced the materials and behavior that are criminal even if the participants are consenting adults. Two categories of behavior that had previously been criminal regardless of consent—pornography and sodomy—were the subject of liberalizing trends in the last third of the twentieth century. Most pornographic communication was decriminalized in the United States by judicial action and in other developed nations by judicial, administrative, and some legislative changes (Hawkins & Zimring, 1989). A number of American states formally decriminalized both heterosexual and homosexual sodomy, and the U.S. Supreme Court announced a constitutional ban on the criminal enforcement of such prohibitions in *Lawrence v. Texas*, 123 S. Ct. 1512 (2003). There were no new categories of sex offenses created during this period, although the general decriminalization of pornography led to special legislation and enforcement efforts in the area of child pornography.

While the number of criminal prohibitions of sexual conduct did not increase, the legal apparatus for discovering, punishing, and controlling sex offenders expanded substantially. Laws mandating compulsory reporting of all sorts of child abuse by physicians, teachers, and social workers were one major new weapon in the campaign against child sexual as well as physical abuse (West's Ann. Cal. Penal Code § 11165.7; N.Y. McKinney's Social Services Law § 413). A range of other new methods of control became law including recording and citizen notification (Megan's Laws), providing for civil commitment for some classes of sex offenders at the end of prison terms, authorizing the administration of chemical castration medications designed to incapacitate sexual arousal and performance as conditions of parole or probation, and lengthening prison terms for some classes of sexual offenders.

The procedures for securing rape convictions were also broadly amended to prohibit the impeachment of complainants by evidence of prior consenting sexual conduct with others (Okla. Stat. Ann. § 2412; N.J. Stat. Ann. § 2A:84A-32.1; Idaho Code § 18-6105; Minn. Stat. Ann. § 609.347; Kan. Stat. Ann. § 21-3525). And special adjustments were made in many states to liberalize conditions for hearing child witnesses without full-scale courtroom confrontations with the defendant and his attorney (Ky. Rev. Stat. § 431.600; La. Rev. Stat. Ann. § 440.4; N.J. Stat. Ann. § 2A:84A-32.4). These procedural changes have all been in the direction of facilitating prosecution and conviction of offenders. The new consequences associated with the sex crime category have been uniformly toward more social control and special strategies for the control and isolation of sex offenders.

Figure 2.6 traces trends in arrests for the three major categories of sex offenses during 1975–2000. The 1975 volume of arrests for all three categories is stated as 100 to allow clear illustration of trends. The figure depicts how trends over time for the different categories of arrest are similar for the first twenty years and then diverge modestly. The volume of arrests reported for all three categories increases modestly until the early 1990s, with rape arrests peaking at 50 percent over the 1975 volume in 1991, prostitution staying near its peak volume for the period 1985–1991, and the arrest volume for other sexual assaults reaching 168 percent of its beginning level in 1991 and 1992. But rape arrests drop in the mid-1990s with the general crime decline, and are only 3 percent above their beginning volume in 2000. Prostitution arrests drop also, but to a level 28 percent higher than the arrest volume in 1975. The arrest volume for the "other sexual assault" category remains high throughout the 1990s, within 15 percent of its peak rate and almost

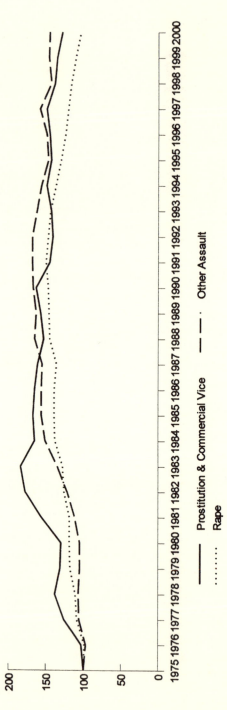

Figure 2.6. Trends in arrests in U.S. for sex offenses during 1975–2000.
Source: U.S. Department of Justice, 1976–2000.

Prostitution & Commercial Vice   Other Assault

⋯⋯⋯ Rape

half again the arrest volume in 1975. Yet these variations in arrest volume are quite modest over the entirety of the period, especially when compared with the volatility of imprisonment levels.

Figure 2.7 traces the trend in prison inmates incarcerated for rape and for other sexual assaults during 1980–1997. Again, the 1980 total for each offense is stated as 100 to show trends. Prostitution and commercial vice are not included because they do not account for a significant proportion of the prison population.

The trends shown in figure 2.7 are of a different scale than the arrest numbers in figure 2.6. During the years after 1980, the total number of persons imprisoned for rape doubles from 13,200 in 1980 to 27,500 in 1997. Controlling for the increase in the adult population, the prison population of convicted rapists was about 80 percent higher in 1997 than in 1980. Meanwhile, the number of persons imprisoned for the heterogeneous "other sexual assault" category expanded from 7,300 in 1980 to over 64,000 in 1997, a growth of just under 800 percent in seventeen years. In 1980, there were approximately two rapists in U.S. state prisons for each person incarcerated for other sexual assault. By 1997, more than twice as many persons were in prison for other sexual assaults as for rape. The growth rate of persons incarcerated for the "other sexual assault" category was four times as large as for rape, and 80 percent of the 71,200 additional sex prisoners added to U.S. prisons between 1980 and 1997 were in the "other sexual assault" category.

The phenomenal growth of the heterogeneous "other sexual assault" category would in more normal eras be stunning evidence of changing priority in the prosecution and punishment of the most serious of nonrape sex offenders, but the period between 1980 and 1997 was no normal period for imprisonment in the United States. Figure 2.8 thus compares incarceration trends for the two sex offenses with the overall growth pattern for other offenses.

What figure 2.8 adds is some control for the general expansion of state prisoners during the years after 1980. Even though the non-sex-crime prison population expands by almost 200 percent over the period 1980–1997, the volume of other sex crime prisoners grows almost three times as fast. This suggests that only part of the sharp increase in sex-offender prisoners can be attributed to the greater tendency to use the prison sanction against all criminal threats. About two-thirds of the growth in prisoners in this group is in excess of the general get-tough trend.

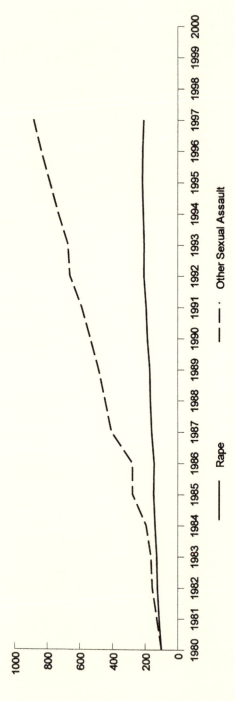

Figure 2.7. Trends in U.S. prisoners incarcerated in state prisons for sex offenses during 1980–1997

Sources: Bureau of Justice Statistics, *Historical Statistics on Prisoners in State and Federal Correctional Institutions, 1925–1986;* BJS, *Prisoners in State and Federal Correctional Institutions,* vols. 1977 & 1978; BJS, *Key Facts at a Glance, Correctional Populations, 1980–2000 Profile of State Prison Inmates,* 1974; BJS, *Correctional Populations in the U.S.,* 1986; BJS, *Correctional Populations in the United States,* 1997, table 1.13; BJS, *Correctional Populations in the United States,* 1993, figure 16.

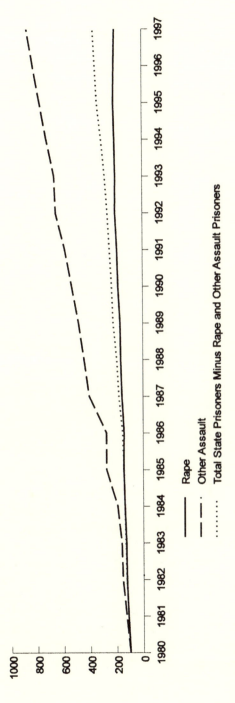

Figure 2.8. Comparison of trends in U.S. prisoners incarcerated for sex and nonsex offenses during 1980–1997

Sources: Bureau of Justice Statistics, *Correctional Populations in the U.S.,* 1986; BJS, *Correctional Populations in the U.S.,* 1997, table 1.13; BJS, *Correctional Populations in the U.S.,* 1993, figure 16; BJS, *Historical Statistics on Prisoners in State and Federal Institutions, 1925–1986;* BJS, *Correctional Populations in the U.S.,* 1987, 1988, 1989.

Rape

Other Assault

Total State Prisoners Minus Rape and Other Assault Prisoners

Chapter 3

The Juvenile Sex Offender

This chapter focuses on the measurement and meaning of sex crimes committed by children and adolescents in the United States. The starting point for this analysis is not arrest statistics or survey research, however, but rather a fundamental distinction in U.S. law between minors and adults that has profound impact not only on the rate of adolescent criminal sexual conduct but on the nature of the conduct that is considered unlawful. The objective of the criminal law regarding the sexual conduct of adults is regulatory. Even at its prohibitory high watermark, Anglo-American law never sought to forbid sexual intercourse between consenting spouses, and current legal policy allows most consensual sex between competent adults. Among the 200 million persons over eighteen in the United States, there are tens of millions of acts of sexual intercourse each week, and most of these are not violations of any criminal code.

For children and younger adolescents, however, the aim of the criminal law is to prohibit interpersonal sexual conduct completely. The Idaho Penal Code provisions discussed in chapter 1 make any "lewd conduct" with a minor under age sixteen a felony offense punishable by up to life imprisonment. For anyone under sixteen, and for all of those in dating relationships with persons under sixteen, the law's objective is to prevent interpersonal genital contact. Every state in the nation has enacted criminal statutes prohibiting sexual intercourse with girls under one age-of-consent threshold (typically age eighteen or sixteen) and lewd conduct statutes prohibiting sexual conduct with boys and girls under lower fixed ages. So the penal law attempts to provide restrictions on the partners and places of consensual sex involving adults, but attempts to forbid interpersonal genital conduct for children and younger adolescents.

It would be difficult to overstate the difference between a legal effort to channel or regulate sexual activities and a legal effort to prohibit them. For those under the relevant ages of consent, all of the fruit on the sexual tree is forbidden—sex must either be avoided or the criminal law will be violated by the minor, her partner, or both. While the choice for adults is between allowed and prohibited sex partners and practices, the choice for those under the age of sexual majority is often between prohibited sexual contacts and no interpersonal sexual contacts. In the specialized language of American juvenile justice, sexual contacts for the very young can be regarded as "status offenses," forbidden because of the immaturity of one of the participants (Teitelbaum, 2002).

Because the law prohibits so many more of available sexual outlets of the young, one would expect to find that the rate of sex offending would be higher for younger teens than for adults, and that the proportion of teen sex offending that was not apparently linked to abnormal sexual tastes or orientations would also be much higher than for adult offenders. Since adults have more noncriminal sexual outlets available to them, they would be expected to choose sexual partners forbidden to them less frequently than young persons, for whom all sexual activity, and sex with most of their closest companions, would be criminal. When an adult targets a prohibited sexual partner, it is often because of a special preference for that type of person.

This chapter is divided into three parts. The first provides a description of the incidence and prevalence of juvenile sex offenses—the amount of offending, the type of offending, and the role of discretion in creating a wide gap between the number and types of offenses that could provoke a legal response and the number and type of offenses that become official statistics. The second part provides data on the extent to which juvenile sex offenders are re-arrested for sex offenses later in their juvenile careers or in early adulthood. The chapter's third part addresses the extent to which juveniles who are arrested for sex offenses display the characteristics that many believe are common in adult sex offenders: psychological abnormality, fixed and deviant sexual preferences, and high rates of sexual recidivism. A concluding note distinguishes among three different types of juvenile sex offenders who require different legal system responses.

The Prevalence and Incidence of Juvenile Sex Offending

There are two methods for estimating the level of criminal sexual conduct by juveniles, and they tell two quite different stories about the magnitude of adolescent sexual behavior and its most common patterns. Official statistics produce modest numbers of youths arrested for sex crimes, while survey research suggests that much larger proportions of the youth population are involved in law-violating sexual behavior.

Arrest Data: The Official Story

The first approach is to use statistics on arrests reported by the police, data parallel to that we explored in chapter 2 for adult offenses. Figure 3.1 launches our review of the statistics on juvenile sex arrests by reproducing the volume of arrests for the three main categories of sex offenses as compiled by the Federal Bureau of Investigation's Uniform Crime Reports.

Taking the year 2000 data as representative of current figures, we find that the total number of rape arrests of persons younger than eighteen is just under 3,000, while the volume of "other sex offenses" is more than 11,000. As with the adults, more than three-fourths of the total in both potentially serious sex arrest categories is to be found in the heterogeneous "other sex offenses" category. Unlike adult arrest patterns, where almost 40 percent of total sex arrests were for commercial vice, only 6 percent of the minors arrested were accused of commercial vice crimes. A plausible reason for this pattern is that when older patrons pay underage sex partners or procure for them, the adult is considered the predator and the child (victim) is not arrested.

The fact that there is one forcible rape arrest for every four "other of-fense" arrests, close to the adult ratio, is a mild surprise because the broader prohibition of nonforcible sexual conduct should produce a much larger preponderance of nonforce arrests if the prohibition on sex with willing peers is being enforced. That the ratio of arrests for nonforcible sexual conduct to arrests for forcible rape is not greater is one indication (of many) that the legal prohibitions on peer sex among minors are not extensively enforced.

Figure 3.2 gives another view of the extent of law enforcement responses to youth's sexual behavior by comparing the proportion of total arrests for a variety of offenses that involve persons under eighteen. Because the majority of those who have sex with partners under sixteen years old are them-selves under eighteen, any broad enforcement of a prohibition of genital sex by young adolescents should result in juveniles' having a larger share of total sex arrests than arrests in other crime categories.

Yet the figures show that the percentages of under-eighteen offenders arrested for sex offenses are *less* than those for major property crimes like

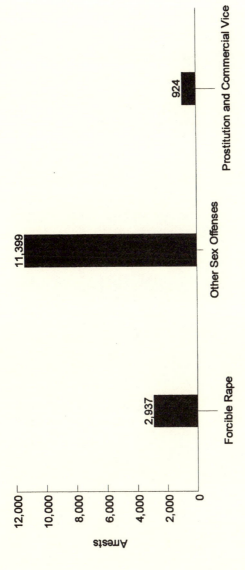

Figure 3.1. U.S. arrests of persons under eighteen for three types of sex crime during 2000

Source: U.S. Department of Justice, 2000, table 38, p. 226.

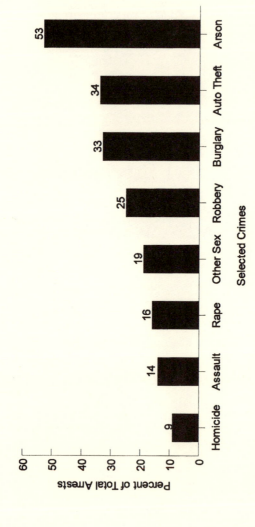

Figure 3.2. Percentage distribution for selected crimes of U.S. arrests of persons under eighteen during 2000

Source: U.S. Department of Justice, 2000, p. 236.

robbery, burglary, and auto theft, and are a fraction of the 53 percent of all arson arrest that involve juveniles. Further, sex arrests are a smaller fraction of total juvenile arrests than of adult arrests. Juvenile rape arrests make up .79 percent of juvenile Part 1 arrests (the adult figure is 1.2 percent), and juvenile arrests for all sex offenses account for 1 in 100 total nontraffic arrests (the adult figure is 1 in 70) (Uniform Crime Reports, 2000). The puzzle here is that kids have twice the rate of total burglary arrests without any special legal liability to account for their inflated share. Yet, compared to adults, many more of the potential sexual contacts of a sixteen year old are prohibited by law. Why is this greater liability not reflected in the younger group's having a larger proportion of total arrests?

One further puzzle in the official statistics on juvenile sex arrests concerns the age distribution of these arrests within the juvenile court ages. The typical pattern for juvenile crime is that those arrested for serious offenses are more often the oldest juveniles (Zimring, 1998, fig. 2.2, p. 22). Figure 3.3 illustrates the pattern of arrests by age for the two major sex-crime categories and for robbery and burglary. The focus in this figure is on the pattern of arrest proneness during the teen years. For each offense the figure assigns the arrest rate per 100,000 at age twenty the value 100, and then shows the arrest rate for each age under twenty as its percentage. So if the rate per 100,000 of burglary arrests at age twenty is 500, and the rate at age ten is 114, the figure shows the age twenty rate as 100 and expresses the age ten rate as proportional to that number, in this case 23 percent. The effect of this measure is to show only the variation in pattern of arrests by age. Because the FBI only reports arrests for multiple year aggregates under age fourteen, I divide these arrests by the number of age groups in the category, assuming each year contributed an equal proportion.

For robbery, the arrest rate for the youngest group in the population is only 7 percent of that for twenty-year-olds; thirteen- and fourteen-year-olds have arrest rates equal to 42 percent of the age twenty rate, but then arrest rates climb to 98 percent by age sixteen and peak at 138 percent at age eighteen. There is a significant increase in arrest rate for each year up to eighteen, a common trend for offenses of violence.

The pattern for burglary is typical for property crimes. Rates start at 23 percent of the age twenty rate, climb steadily to age seventeen, and peak at age eighteen at 158 percent. There is then a sharp drop to arrest risks at age twenty.

The forcible rape pattern resembles that of robbery, starting at 12 percent of the age twenty rate for those twelve and younger, climbing to just over half the age twenty volume at ages thirteen and fourteen, then peaking

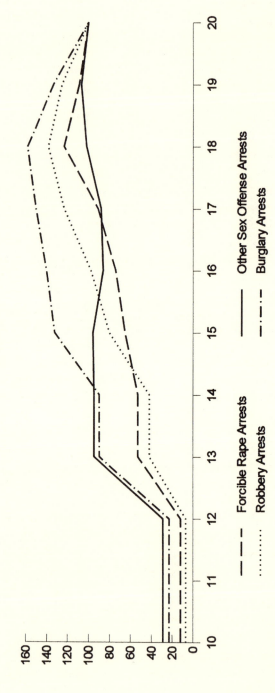

Figure 3.3. Patterns of arrests among teenagers during 2000
Sources: U.S. Department of Justice, 2000; and U.S. Census, 2000.

at age eighteen but with a rate only 23 percent higher than that found at age twenty. This "low peak" pattern is typical for violence offenses. The forcible rape pattern does have a higher relative rate in the youngest years, with thirteen- and fourteen-year-olds arrested at over half the age twenty rate. The median age of arrest for all under-eighteen rape suspects is fifteen, while the under-eighteen median age for robbery is sixteen (U.S. Department of Justice, 2001, p. 246).

The pattern in figure 3.3 for "other sex offenses" is dramatically different. First, the arrest rates are relatively high at very young ages: rates are already at 29 percent of the age twenty rate and 26 percent of the highest recorded rate in the ten- to twelve-year-old age categories. Burglary, the next highest crime for ten- to twelve-year-olds, has an arrest rate in that age group that is only 15 percent of its peak adolescent rate. Even more striking is the fact that the arrest rate for these other sex crimes is 95 percent of the peak adolescent rate by ages thirteen and fourteen. The next highest youth concentration at thirteen and fourteen (other than arson) is burglary, which has an arrest rate that is 57 percent of its peak at age eighteen. The arrest concentrations in the youngest FBI age categories are twice as high for "other sex offenses" as for burglary. The median age of all males arrested for "other sex crimes" in 2001 was fourteen compared to age sixteen for the robbery youth group (U.S. Department of Justice, 2001, p. 246).

A second notable feature of the "other sex offenses" arrest patterns is that there really is no peak year for this charge. Offense rates measured by arrest are almost as high at age thirteen and fourteen as at any older age, and, indeed, figure 3.3 depicts them as slightly higher at thirteen and fourteen than at ages sixteen and seventeen. The only other offense category with a similar arrest pattern is arson, for which the arrests are concentrated in the early teen years (see figure 3.2).

Relatively high arrest rates for sex offenses other than rape are present in early adolescence, and there is no climb in the rate of "other sex offenses" during the midteen years to parallel the higher incidence and prevalence of sexual activity at ages fifteen and sixteen. Whatever makes boys vulnerable to arrest for this crime is present quite early—at the very beginnings of interpersonal sexual experience—and does not increase as rates of sexual contact increase through the teen years.

There are also indications that the arrests of many younger offenders are based on less serious charges than arrests of older juveniles or adults. Details on arrests reported to the FBI are not available through the Uniform Crime Reports system, but a special statistical instrument used in several states—the National Incident-Based Reporting System (NIBRS)—breaks noncommercial sex arrests into four categories: forcible rape, forcible sodomy, sexual assault, and forcible fondling. Howard Synder of the National Center for Juvenile Justice (NCJJ) compiled the NIBRS data to show, as illustrated in figure 3.4, the percentage of each age group's sex arrests classified as falling in the least serious category of "forcible fondling."

Charges of forcible fondling account for less than one-third of the young adult arrests reported in figure 3.4, while completed forcible rape accounts for more than half of the arrest volume for every age above sixteen. By contrast, the least serious fondling charge makes up more than 60 percent of the large volume of arrests of those twelve and under, and then steadily diminishes with each year of advancing age to age twenty.

The explanation for this puzzling pattern is that arrests and court cases mainly pertain to a small and unrepresentative segment of teen sex behavior that violates the law. While sexual contacts under age sixteen are typically prohibited, the majority of actual arrest cases involve boys in their early to midteens who have sexual contact with much younger children, usually girls.

The low incidence and selectivity of arrests for nonforcible sex crimes are apparent when official arrest rates are compared with the self-reported behaviors of boys and girls of the same ages. The odds that an adolescent male will be arrested for one of the nonrape sex offenses is almost exactly 1 in 1,000 per year at ages fifteen and sixteen. The odds that male youths of that age will have participated in legally prohibited acts with girls under sixteen in states with Idaho-style lewd conduct laws are probably about 50 percent, and the rate of sexual contact per year per boy is much greater than one. So if arrests were distributed evenly across the range of underage sexual conduct, being apprehended for such an act would be the equivalent of winning fourth prize in a lottery, somewhere between 1 in 1,000 and 1 in 20,000.

But the broadest study of victim characteristics in cases that result in arrest shows how selective the arrest process must be. Figure 3.5 uses the NIBRS data to show the age distributions of victims involved in juvenile sex cases leading to arrest in those jurisdictions attempting to compile offender-based transaction records.

The median age of a victim of a sexual incident leading to arrest in the NIBRS sample is eleven, far younger than the distribution by age of children and young adolescents involved in sexual activity in dating and relationship settings. The skew by age suggests that police and courts usually do not attempt to enforce prohibitions against consensual near-peer sexual

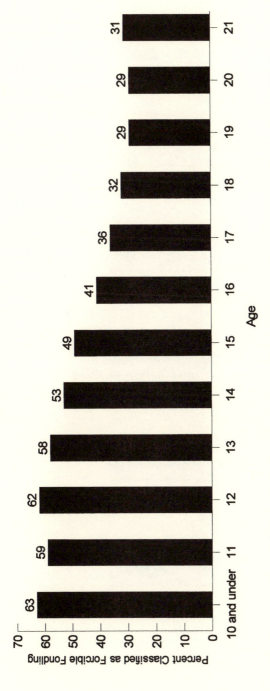

Figure 3.4. Percentage of total arrests of juveniles for sex offenses that was reported as "forcible fondling" during 1991–1996
Source: McCurley, Sickmund, & Snyder, 2003.

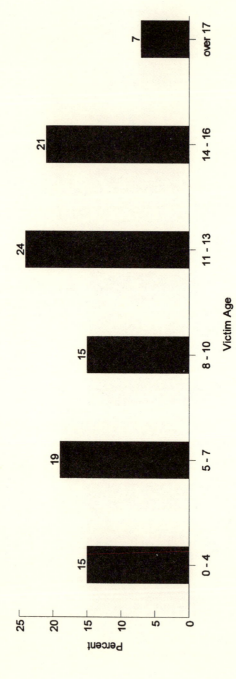

Figure 3-5. Age distribution for victims of accused juvenile sex offenders during 1991–1996
Source: McCurley, Sickmund, & Snyder, 2003.

activity, but do attempt to stop what they consider child sexual abuse even when the offenders are also very young.

Table 3.1 uses the same NIBRS study data to show the age distribution of victims separately for each age group of offenders. The majority of young child victims were involved with the very youngest of the children and youths who were arrested. While 78 percent of those victimized by arrested kids ten and under were younger than nine years old, only 13 percent of the reported victims of seventeen-year-olds were under nine. Sixty percent of all victims under the age of nine were involved with offenders under fourteen, and 88 percent were victimized by offenders under the age of fifteen.

JUVENILE SEX CRIME AS LETHAL VIOLENCE. Cases in which juvenile sex offenders kill their victims are worth special analysis for two reasons. First, sex crimes that cost the victim her life are the most serious on the sex-crime spectrum, the most heinous offenses fueling the public's fear and outrage, and prompting the enactment of such statutory measures such as Megan's Laws and the federal Jacob Wetterling Act. Second, the death rate from juvenile sex offending is an important way to help measure whether the thousands of nonlethal sex arrests involving juveniles reflect the same volume of crimes and the same type of acts as the sex crimes of older offenders. The death rate from juvenile versus adult sex offending is one good measure of the dangerousness of the activity.

The good news is that sex crimes by juveniles that result in the victim's death are very rare events. At the time of this writing, the most recent FBI Supplemental Homicide Report data is for 1998 and 1999. Nationwide, during these two years, there were nine known sex-crime killings involving at least one juvenile offender, four to five cases per year in a nation approaching 300 million in population.

There are two reasons for this small number of sex-crime fatalities involving juveniles. The first is that the total volume of sex-crime homicide identified in these FBI statistics is quite low. The total death rate from sex crimes that resulted in an arrest was 160 for 1998–1999, as reported in chapter 2. But even with this low rate of total homicide, juveniles do not commit anywhere near the numbers of killings one would expect from their share of the sex-offense arrest statistics. Figure 3.6 compares the proportion that are juveniles among the total arrests for forcible rape, for other sex felonies, and for killings that result from them. While 16 percent of rape arrests and 19 percent of other sex felony arrests are under age eighteen, the same age group accounts for less than 6 percent of all arrests for killings that result from the same two categories of sex crime. If the juvenile arrest share is

Table 3.1. Age Distribution of Victims by Age of Offender, NIBRS Jurisdictions, 1991–1996 (%)

Victim age	Offender Age							
	10 and under	11	12	13	14	15	16	17
5 and under	46	39	34	27	22	17	10	7
6–8	32	33	25	24	18	16	9	6
9–11	15	19	17	17	16	13	11	9
12	1	3	9	8	8	7	8	4
13	1	3	7	12	12	12	13	12
14	1	1	3	6	12	12	14	16
15	—	1	1	3	5	11	13	15
16	—	—	—	1	2	5	10	11
17	—	—	—	—	1	2	4	7
18 and over	1	—	3	1	4	5	9	13
Sample size	1,323	612	990	1,633	1,950	1,946	1,913	1,955

Source: Data provided by Howard Snyder, NCJJ.

so high in these crimes, why are juveniles arrested for fewer than one in seventeen sex-crime killings?

One reason for inflation of the juvenile crime share when arrest statistics are compiled is that youths are more likely to be arrested in groups, so that juveniles account for a larger percentage of arrests than of offenders responsible for crime. Howard Snyder shows that while juveniles totaled 16 percent of all rape arrests, for example, they were responsible for only 12 percent of the rape incidents that the arrest statistics covered. But that still leaves a large gap between the 12 percent of rape incidents and 5.6 percent of all sex-offense killings. And there is no evidence that group arrest phenomena are a good explanation for the 19 percent of all nonrape arrests, which represent 80 percent of the total of juvenile arrests for sex crimes. Why the gap?

There are two other plausible explanations for this pattern. One is quantitative and the other qualitative. The quantitative explanation is that adults escape detection for predatory sex crimes more easily than juveniles, so that the adult share of sex crimes is much closer to their 94 percent of all sex-crime killings than their 84 percent share of rape arrests and 81 percent share of other sex-crime arrests. If this is the principal explanation for the gap between arrests for killings and those for nondeadly sex offenses, then

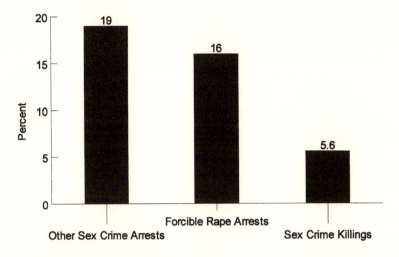

Figure 3.6. Comparison of percentages of U.S. arrests of juveniles under eighteen for different sex crimes during 1998–1999
Source: U.S. Department of Justice, 2000.

the juvenile share of all nonconsensual sex crimes is less—much less—than has been estimated. Of course, there are also millions of uncounted acts of consensual peer sex by adolescents that are technical violations of the criminal law, but these are probably not dangerous.

The qualitative explanation for the gap between the juvenile share of arrests for fatal versus nonfatal sex offenses is that the offenses juveniles commit under the same classifications as adults are in fact both qualitatively different than adult acts and less life threatening.

My guess is that both explanations contribute to this fascinating comparison, but that the quantitative explanation is the more important of the two. The chances that adolescent sex offenses will result in arrest are probably much greater than the chances that adult sex offenses will. Where so few hard statistics can be obtained on the danger of juvenile sex offenses, this particular data set deserves further scrutiny now that the discrepancy between general and lethal sex-crime arrests has been discovered.

Two other statistical comparisons concerning juvenile sex killings provide further data on the relationship between juvenile sex offending and juvenile violence. In 1998–1999, offenders under eighteen were arrested for a total of 2,168 homicides. The total number of sex-offense killings (nine) was less than one-half of 1 percent of all youth homicides. To the extent that policy priorities should be motivated by reducing adolescent homicide, the sex cases are less than a drop in the bucket. By comparison, the number of those under age eighteen who were arrested for robbery homicide during the same two years was 373, approximately forty-one times as many as the sex-crime homicide arrests.

The final statistic that helps place sex killings by juveniles in context concerns the risk of homicide that juvenile offenders pose for young children. The large number of child victims in sex-offense arrest studies (see table 3.1) raises the question of the sex-offender share of juvenile killings of young children. The FBI arrest statistics show that in 1998–1999 juvenile suspects were blamed by the police for 112 killings of children under ten years of age in the United States. Only two cases, or less than 2 percent of the total, involved sex offenses. For children and youth from ten to seventeen, the FBI reports three more sex cases in an additional total of 438 killings, so the sex-offense share drops to less than 1 percent of all children and youths killed by juvenile offenders. The overlap between juvenile sex offenses and life-threatening violence is by any measure quite small. If the risk of death that sex offenders pose for children is the main concern, adolescent sex crimes are a tiny percentage of the problem of adolescent violence.

Survey Research on Sexual Experience

A second method for estimating the prevalence of law violation in teen sexual conduct is survey research. As part of a large and carefully constructed survey of teen health risks, the results reported in figure 3.7 show the percentage of teens thirteen through seventeen years old who have engaged in interpersonal genital play and sexual intercourse. The two categories of reported sexual conduct in the figure are sexual intercourse, the act required for the offense of statutory rape, and interpersonal genital play (the question asked was "Ever touch another's genitals?"), to correspond to the definition of lewd conduct in most statutes.

The increase in sexual experience is orderly and substantial over time, with the patterns for boys and girls paralleling each other nicely. By age fourteen, more than one-third of respondents report genital play and about one-fifth have started having sexual intercourse. By age sixteen, over 40 percent of both sexes report intercourse, and that rises to 55 percent for both boys and girls at age seventeen—which in the case of female participation many states would still regard as statutory rape. With an age boundary of fourteen, more than one-third of both boys and girls have been victims of lewd conduct as the law defines that term. If partners are the same age or younger, at least 50 percent of all boys at some period of adolescence have committed sexual felonies with girls under age eighteen. So a strict legal

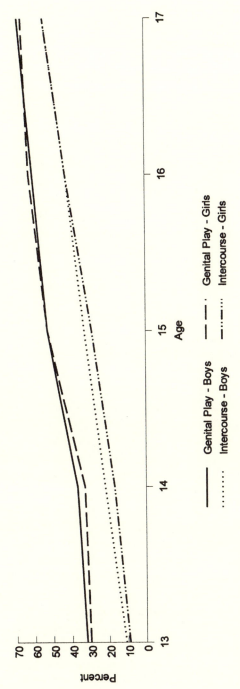

Figure 3.7. Prevalence in U.S. of sexual intercourse and genital play by age during 2000
Source: U.S. Department of Health and Welfare, National Institute of Child Health and Human Development, *National Longitudinal Study of Adolescent Health* (2000).

standard would criminalize conduct that is, statistically speaking, quite normal among teen populations.

It has already been shown, however, that the victimization pattern for actual teen sex arrests usually involves younger children. So the law in practice, at least in most cases, is concerned with child abuse and force. But a large gap between the formal criteria of the criminal law and the actual standards of most law enforcement agencies can generate problems. In the first place, some teen sex behavior that most communities and law enforcement agencies would not process as criminal may nevertheless lead to arrest and punishment. It is small consolation to a seventeen-year-old arrested for consensual sex with his sixteen-year-old girlfriend that most police officials and judges would not press charges. This is particularly problematic for kids who live in high-visibility social control settings such as group homes or institutional facilities. A large gap between the law in practice (in most cases) and the law on the books can lead to a double standard in the application of the statute.

Michael Caldwell describes how such a double standard may arise in cases of peer teen sex in Wisconsin:

> In Wisconsin this activity falls under the mandatory child abuse reporting laws because the acts are statutorily defined as felony sexual abuse of a child, regardless of the age of the offender. As a result, juvenile residential treatment programs routinely report consensual teen sexual intercourse to the authorities. Often both youth are charged with felony sexual assault of a child, an adjudication that carries mandatory sex offender registration for at least 15 years after the end of the juvenile supervision. [I have] an association with a small juvenile sex offender treatment program in a secured juvenile corrections facility. Of the last 25 admissions to that program, 11 had been adjudicated on this type of offense. (Caldwell, 2002, p. 292)

It is also true that relying on statutes that prohibit genital touching under age sixteen or that legally define sexual intercourse at seventeen as statutory rape provides a misleading impression of social norms. The law is much stricter than social norms. When groups like the Task Force on Juvenile Sexual Offenders suggest that legal definitions be regarded as the standard of sexual abuse (see chapter 4), the nature of the current statutory framework is bound to result in definitions of sexual abuse that are unrealistically overinclusive.

ASKING THE WRONG QUESTION. Just as systematic analysis of representative samples of adolescent sex offenders is rare, there have been no extensive efforts to compare the characteristics and motivations of adolescent sex offenders with different types of adult offenders. Instead, retrospective reports of adult offenders have been used as evidence that many pathological conditions start young. The foreword to a literature review published by the Office of Juvenile Justice and Delinquency Prevention in 2001 states: "Perhaps even more disturbing are the indications that one in two adult sex offenders began sexually abusive behavior as a juvenile" (Righthand & Welch, 2001, p. iii). And the 1993 revised report of the National Task Force on Juvenile Sexual Offending asserts that a key finding that justifies broad-based intervention in adolescent conduct was "in part based on the recognition that as many as 60–80% of adult offenders reported offending as adolescents." (National Adolescent Perpetrator Network, 1993, p. 5). But the Task Force equivocates on the importance of this data: "Although the retrospective data from chronic adult offenders *cannot* be projected onto all sexually abusive youth as a prediction, it does indicate an 'at risk' condition, and early intervention is clearly indicated" (p. 5; italics in original).

In fact, knowing what proportion of later sexual offenders committed an offense in adolescence tells us next to nothing about how likely it is that certain teen sexual behavior leads to later offending behavior, and therefore presents a very weak case for early intervention for the majority of teen sex offenses. The important issue is not how many later chronic offenders started young, it is what proportion of a group of young offenders presents a significant risk of further trouble. That is an issue that requires studying a cohort of younger offenders over time to determine the base rate of later offending and whether the group that will later get in trouble can be predicted with any efficiency. If the rate of juvenile offending is high enough, 60 percent of all serious adult offenders might have some teen history of offenses, but fewer than 1 in 100 teen offenders might need intervention. Unless early intervention is costless and benign, it is the proportion of current offenders who require treatment that is crucial in the case for early intervention.

The problems of basing a case for early intervention on retrospective studies is compounded by the fact that the statistical evidence for finding precursors to adult offending in teen behavior is based on self-report studies. The only specific finding in the articles cited by the 1993 Task Force comes from a study of incarcerated adults in Connecticut and Florida, where the offenders were asked to remember their age when they first committed sexual assault involving force or a child target. "Forty-seven percent reported a first assault between ages 8 and 18" (Groth, Longo, & McFadin, 1982). This analysis cites a mean age of first behavior in the teens for sexual assault, but reports the mean age as 23 and 24 for child molesters. There is no indication of how many of these behaviors or offenders came to official attention, so there is no reason to suppose that 47 percent of eventual offenders could be identified through juvenile contacts, or even 20 percent. The proportion of offenders that did generate official records is never reported, nor is there any other basis for estimating from this type of research what fraction of identified adult offenders came to the attention of juvenile authorities. So there is no indication of what proportion of later chronic sex offenders would be captured in any program that treated even 100 percent of known adolescent offenders.

The indications that many later chronic offenders began to manifest offending behavior as teens is a much more persuasive reason for seeking to identify high-risk teen subpopulations than it is for the extensive treatment of all adolescent offenders. The presence of a small high-risk population in the larger mass of teen offenders is a much better argument for mass screening than it is for mass treatment. But the report of the 1993 Task Force seems to use the "at risk" condition as an argument for treating all teen offenders. That a document that argues for intensive monitoring and follow-up for all youths in the system (see, e.g., National Adolescent Perpetrator Network, 1993, Assumptions 77 and 78) cites no evidence on recidivism rates or offense seriousness is astonishing. That the report apparently assumes that the persistence in sexual abuse of an unknown fraction of the adolescent offender population is a sufficient justification for plenary intervention is not an encouraging sign. This 1993 report is considered in detail in chapter 4.

Is the Juvenile Offender a Sexual Danger?

To assess the future dangerousness of the juvenile sex offenders who come to the attention of public authorities, careful follow-up studies of broad samples of identified teen offenders are required. The more representative of identified offenders each study population is, the more reliable will be its data regarding the character and risks of known juvenile sex offenders. This section reviews several studies that attempt to trace broad samples of adolescent sex offenders.

Texas Youth Commission

One recent recidivism study by the Texas Youth Commission followed a cohort of seventy-two young offenders who together represented all those released in one year after being detained in state correctional facilities for having committed juvenile sex crimes. The study traced re-arrest data for the first three years after release. But this is not a representative sample of Texas juvenile sex offenders because all those offenders who managed to avoid state correctional commitment are not included. The "institutions only" release group might be expected to have higher recidivism rates than other juvenile offenders for two reasons. First, other studies have shown that young offenders released from institutions have higher re-arrests than those from community-based programs (Schram, Milloy, & Rowe, 1991; Gfellner, 2000). Second, whenever judges have a discretionary choice between institutions and alternative placements, they will assign those they regard as posing the greatest risks to the institutional program.

Three years after release from the state institutions, a total of three of the seventy-two offenders had been re-arrested for a sexual offense—a cumulative re-arrest rate of 4.2 percent (Liedecke and Marbibi, 2000). Four years of postrelease data was available for one subgroup of the released population, and the reported re-arrest rate increased to 8 percent; but that increase was the result of only one new arrest among this subgroup, which was only one-third as large as the original.

Some arrest statistics can put the Texas data in context. As mentioned, the seventy-two offenders followed by the Texas Youth Commission were the total number released in one year from Youth Commission facilities after serving a sentence for a sex offense. The study finds that the expected volume of arrests per year for this group is one per year averaged over a three-year follow-up. In 2000, the total number of arrests in Texas for rape and other sex offenses was 7,080 (Department of Justice, 2001, pp. 278–279). So this cohort of released inmates were responsible for one-seventieth of 1 percent of the sex-crime problem in Texas, if their share of arrests is equal to their share of sex crimes committed.

The low rate of re-offense found in Texas is not a surprise. The grandfather of all outcome studies of juvenile sex offenders was published in 1943 by Lewis Doshay, a psychiatrist long associated with New York City's Children's Court. His sample of 256 males was composed of "all instances of male sex delinquency found in the clinics of the children's courts of the various boroughs of New York City" for six years beginning in 1928. Only boys with IQs under 70 were excluded from the sample. About 40 percent of the juveniles in this group had committed sex offenses but no other delinquent acts, while the remainder of the group had both sex and nonsex delinquencies in their juvenile records (Doshay, 1943, pp. 71–89). The treatments accorded these cases included supervision (for an average of five months) and visits to the court's clinic (an average of two times) (p. 86). The outcome period was not a fixed time after discharge or the age of majority but rather was for the duration of the study period (approximately through 1941), which is described as between six and twelve years after the youth's last treatment at the clinic (p. 1). However, because the study only counts offending after the sixteenth birthday as a re-offense, the "at risk" follow-up period of the study could have been less than six years after that birthday.

Doshay (1943) reports the recidivism rates for the total sample of sex offenders (total sample = 256):

Sex offense   3.1
Other offense   15

The figures point out both the low rates of sex offending in later years and the much higher rates of arrest for other offenses that later studies would also report. What is remarkable is that a study of this importance is not a more prominent part of the discourse about the nature and risk of juvenile sex offending.

The Three-Site Juvenile Court Samples

A study by the National Council on Crime and Delinquency for the federal Office of Juvenile Justice and Delinquency Prevention provided meticulous tracing of all cases referred to juvenile courts for sex offenses during sample periods in three sites: Baltimore, San Francisco, and Lucas County, Ohio (Wiebush, 1996). This project included all sex-crime charges that reached the intake stage of juvenile court in the three sites, so the mix of offenses should vary more in seriousness than the Texas study population. As was true of Dr. Doshay's New York sample, whatever heterogeneity exists in the arrested population should be reflected in the cases covered in this study. According to police reports, the offenses that led to court referral were not trivial: "40–60% of the offenses involved penetration; 25–60% involved the use of force; 36–54% involved (at least) a four-year age differential between the offender and the victim; and 20–36% of the cases involved repeat victimization" (Wiebush, 1996, p. 34).

The measure of recidivism used in this analysis was a re-arrest that resulted in referral to court intake. Figure 3.8 shows the recidivism rates for all three sites for re-arrests for nonsex offenses and re-arrests for sex offenses eighteen months after the initial juvenile court disposition. When the follow-up period was extended by eight months in Baltimore, by one year in Lucas County, and by eleven months in San Francisco, the percentage of youths arrested for nonsex crimes increased in all three locations, but the sex-offense re-arrest rate stayed at 5.5 percent in San Francisco and at 3.2 percent in Lucas County. The re-arrest prevalence for sex offenses rose from 3.3 to 4.2 percent in Baltimore.

The pattern revealed in figure 3.8 is typical of follow-up studies of juveniles arrested for sex offenses. The re-arrest rate for all offenses can be quite high in this period of adolescent development when arrest rates typically peak, but the rate of re-arrest for sex offenses is small. Two years after their court disposition involving a sex charge, the re-arrest rates for sex offenses among the youths in San Francisco and Lucas County were one-eighth the total re-arrest rates in those sites, and less than one-tenth the total arrest rate in Baltimore. Judged by their later arrest histories, these juveniles look much more like undifferentiated delinquents than a specialized risk population. Even a long-term sex re-arrest rate of 4 percent is higher than the arrest rate for sex offenses of juveniles not previously charged with sex crimes; but sex is at most one of many delinquent trajectories for these adolescents. And the extremely high nonsex re-arrest prevalence for these groups makes it less likely that the low prevalence of sex re-arrests can be attributed to any talent this group has for avoiding detection for any crime.

There are two long-range, follow-up studies based on large samples of one segment of juvenile sex offenders. Schram, Milloy, and Rowe (1991) follow juvenile sex offenders in the state of Washington who had centralized state files, without reporting what percentage of total case flow this group represents. In a five-year follow-up, 12 percent of this group were arrested for a sex-related offense and 10 percent were convicted. Sipe, Jensen, and Everett (1998) report a one- to fourteen-year (mean six years) follow-up of 164 offenders with a 9.7 percent re-arrest and conviction rate.

Bremer reports findings from a study of 193 males released from a residential Hennipin County program prior to February 1991 who were followed for postrelease periods ranging from a few months to eight and a half, and averaging just over four years (Bremer, 1992, p. 329, table 4). The author finds a 6 percent reconviction rate in the official follow-up for sex

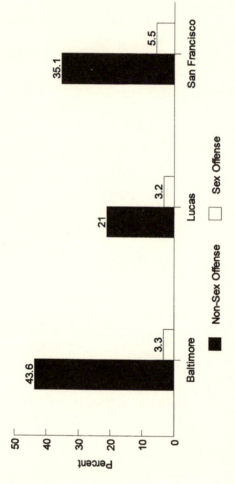

Figure 3.8. Eighteen-month re-arrest rate of juveniles originally charged with sex crimes

Source: Wiebush, 1996, p. 71.

offenses. The study also reports an 11 percent rate of self-reported sexual abuse after treatment although it also claims there were only fifteen acts of sex abuse attributable to the 193 subjects (Bremer, 1992, p. 329). The study population were all released from a residential program designed for "the serious sexual offender" only (p. 327).

Lab, Shields, and Schondel (1993) followed a cohort of young offenders referred for sex-offender treatment screening for an unspecified period up to three years after referral, and report recidivism in 5 out of 155 youths, or 3.2 percent. By contrast, 29 of the 155 youths were re-arrested for nonsex offenses, a 19 percent rate. Gfellner (2000) used country probation records in Manitoba to follow seventy-five offenders and reports a 2.7 percent recidivism rate after several years. The proportion of juvenile sex offender cases to be found in those records and the dispositions and offenses of non-probation-record offenders are not provided.

A variety of clinically identified populations have also been the subject of follow-up studies. These are populations that include some juveniles placed by courts but they are an unspecified share of juvenile sex offenders seen by courts, and are by no means a representative sample of adolescent sex offenders. Where large clinical samples of juvenile sex offenders have been followed, reported recidivism as variously measured ranges from 0 percent (Milloy, 1994) to around 10 percent. The reported recidivism rates for smaller clinical samples range over a wider scale.

There have been two recent efforts at gathering data on juvenile offenders into aggregate categories. Michael Caldwell collected thirteen published studies with details on sexual re-arrests, some of which are representative samples of offenders while others are clinical or institutional subsamples of juvenile offenders. Eleven of the thirteen studies followed seventy-five or more offenders for a median period of three years (Caldwell, 2002, table 1). The total sexual re-arrest prevalence ranged from 1.8 to 12.2 percent, with a median of 4.8 percent. The rate of re-arrest per year of exposure ranged from 0.2 to 4.8 percent, with a median value of 1.6 percent per year. (These are my calculations of rate based on his data.)

Caldwell also reported a group of follow-up studies, often with institutional populations, which used reconviction rates as the failure measure. The median follow-up period for these studies was forty-five months and the median sexual offense failure rate was 10 percent (Caldwell, 2002, table 2). For this group the median prevalence of sex offense per year of exposure was 2.7 percent. If a history of a juvenile sex offense was to be used as a basis for predicting a person's future sex offending, the existing studies surveyed by Caldwell suggest that prediction would be wrong more than nine times out of ten.

Margaret A. Alexander undertook a meta-analysis of studies of treatment that reported on outcomes for over 10,000 sex offenders of a variety of ages and types, including 1,025 juveniles *who completed some form of treatment.* The recidivism rates of treated juveniles were 56 percent of the recidivism rates of similarly treated adult offenders (7.1 vs. 12.5 percent) (see Alexander, 1999, table 1, first row). When adult incest offenders are removed from the comparison, the rate for the rest of adults goes up and the advantage for the juveniles is even more dramatic (Alexander, 1999, table 4).

While the comparison of treated juvenile and adult groups seems justified, both the aggregate risks reported for the juvenile and adult offenders and Alexander's argument that treatment benefits the juveniles are not supported by the data. The aggregate re-arrest rate was computed with only data on those who *completed* treatment. "The current subject pool does not include subjects who dropped out or were terminated during the course of treatment" (Alexander, 1999, p. 103). This is not the proper way to calculate a base expectancy rate. Further, the argument that "juveniles responded well to treatment" (p. 110) cannot be accepted for two reasons. First, there is no untreated control of juveniles, so that the low rate of recidivism may not be a function of intervention effects. Second, with noncompleters screened out, it would not be possible to find an equivalent group of untreated subjects that would be an appropriate comparison to the all-completer treatment group.

The existing data on the general run of juvenile sex offenders provide solid evidence that young offenders are much less likely than adult offenders to commit further sex offenses and that the known rates of sex re-offending for juveniles are also very low in absolute terms. There has been extensive controversy about the relationship between official and actual recidivism rates among adults. There is no empirical evidence that repetitive juvenile sex offenders escape re-arrest to parallel the arguments used to undermine confidence in adult recidivism data as a good measure of the prevalence of adult recidivism. The current studies based on official statistics suggest that re-arrest rates for juveniles are about half those for non-incest-committing adults. But if the major reason why juveniles account for only 5.6 percent of all sex-offense killings is that they are caught more often when they do re-offend than adult offenders, the true difference in recidivism could be much greater than 2 to 1.

Comparative Assessments

In recent years, the psychological literature on juvenile sex-offender populations has begun to compare these groups with other juvenile offenders (see, e.g., Milloy, 1994; Spaccarelli et al., 1997). The two groups generally are quite similar on the measured variables in the reported studies. When sex-offender and non-sex-offender populations in institutions are compared, however, the juvenile sex offenders tend to be younger and have less substantial criminal records, probably a result of the tendency of the courts to commit a larger proportion of serious sex offenders to institutions after a first apprehension.

What is conspicuously missing in the literature is a systematic comparison of juvenile with adult sex offenders, particularly a comparison that uses representative samples of offenders processed through juvenile and criminal justice systems. With so much public policy based on assumptions of continuity between youthful and adult sex offenders, there is a troubling shortage of data and research effort to explore the similarities and differences between child and youthful offenders and adult offenders processed through agencies of criminal justice. The meta-analysis reported by Alexander (1999) compares juvenile and adult treated populations and finds that adult recidivism is almost twice as high, but no data are provided on untreated populations or treatment drop-outs.

A second major failing in the literature on youthful sex offenders is the lack of any studies of clinical characteristics of representative samples of arrested children and adolescents. With very low base expectancy rates of sex-offense recidivism for the entire group of apprehended juvenile sex offenders, the identification of subtypes in the criminal justice population with different symptoms and propensities than the general run of offenders becomes important. Yet while clinicians have proposed subtypologies of adolescent sexual offenders, no comprehensive research has sought to sort the heterogeneous assortment of 15,000 juveniles arrested for sex offenses each year into subgroups of clinical relevance and predictive value to test in systemic studies of recidivism.

Do Adolescent Sex Offenders Fit the Sex-Offender Paradigm?

The last chapter argued that many of the recent policy initiatives directed toward the problem of sex offenders assume four related characteristics of the prototype offender who is the intended target for registration, community notification, chemical interventions, and extended terms as civil or criminal confinement. The four characteristics are psychological sexual abnormality, fixed sexual preferences, a proclivity toward committing sexual crime rather than a wider variety of other offenses, and a high degree of future sexual dangerousness. The extent to which adult offenders fit this pattern is not known, but the situation concerning adolescent offenders is different. When studying representative samples of adolescent sex-law offenders, the data show a pattern of behavior that is almost exactly opposite to the above presumed characteristics—characteristics that underlie much of the statutory law (e.g., Megan's Laws) governing how sexual offenders are treated.

Psychopathology and Juvenile Sex Offending

An important distinction must be made at the outset between problematic behaviors and sexual behavior that is symptomatic of serious emotional disturbances. The literature on treatment of juvenile sex offenders typically distinguishes between normative sexual conduct for youth and abusive behavior (see National Adolescent Perpetrator Network, 1993, p. 5). From that perspective, it can be argued that most arrests of juveniles are due to abusive patterns of behavior and that abusive behavior should be punished in some fashion. The 1993 Task Force on Juvenile Sexual Offending defines abusive behavior as a "law violation" (National Adolescent Perpetrator Network, 1993, p. 6). I explore this approach to the definition of sexual abuse in chapter 4. For now, it is sufficient to note that there is no reason to assume that the presence of legally defined abusive behavior is a clear indication of paraphilia in over 90 percent of youths arrested for sex offending.

The gold standard for the diagnosis of serious sexual dysfunctions is the American Psychiatric Association's *Diagnostic and Statistical Manual*, most recently published in a revised fourth edition in 2000. Using the definitions and diagnostic criteria of DSM-IV, I would guess that fewer than 10 percent of U.S. juveniles who are arrested exhibit any sign of paraphilia, and much of the statistical evidence presented earlier in this chapter is consistent with this finding.

Given the statistical pattern of very young victims in juvenile offending, the most critical category of psychiatric classification for juvenile offenders is pedophilia, defined as "abusive sexual uses of children." Aren't the fourteen- and fifteen-year-old offenders who fondle seven-year-olds exhibiting evidence of a chronic sexual attraction focused on children? The problem with this inference is distinguishing between situations where the choice of a child as target is opportunistic rather than the result of a clear preference. The iron rule established by the DSM-IV is that no sexual conduct can be the basis for a diagnosis unless "[t]he person is at least 16 years of age and at least 5 years older than the prepubescent child or children" (American Psychiatric Association, 2000, p. 572). When this diagnostic criterion is applied to the thousands of arrests reported in the National Incident-Based Reporting System (NIBRS), only 8 percent of the incidents leading to a juvenile arrest would be eligible as evidence of a pedophilia disorder (see table 3.1), and there is no indication of how many of these 8 percent of nonexcluded acts actually do provide substantial indications of child-focused sexual arousal.

There are a number of factors that suggest a minimal presence of extensive psychiatric disorders in juvenile sex-offender populations. The sharp decline in child victims as the arrest populations age demonstrates that child targets do not remain a clear sexual preference for adolescent offenders (see table 3.1). The young victims of young sexual offenders seem most often to be targets of opportunity rather than sexual preference. The low re-arrest rates found even in prison release samples are consistent with nonchronic sexual misconduct, while the very high rates of nonsexual re-arrest make it unlikely that the very low sexual re-arrest rates are a result of skill at avoiding detection.

There is support also for this interpretation in the exploratory literature comparing juvenile sex offenders with other delinquents. The similarities between sexual and nonsexual offenders suggest that both groups are predominately nonclinical populations. The pilot studies that find adolescent sex offenders do not have differential arousal with child sex stimuli while adult offenders do are further evidence that the juvenile offenders are not paraphilic in orientation.

There are, however, some sexual disorders where behavior at earlier ages has diagnostic value, such as fetishes, exhibitionism, and frotteurism, but this behavior is apparently not the basis for many juvenile sexual arrests in the NIBRS and the National Council on Crime and Delinquency (NCCD) samples (see American Psychiatric Association, 2000, pp. 569–579). Juveniles arrested for other sexual crimes might also have clinically significant conditions like fetishism, but the extent to which this occurs is not known.

The available statistics also make short work of theories that juvenile sex offenders specialize in sexual crimes. They do not. Nor is there evidence of the kind of fixed, abnormal sexual preferences that are part of the image of paraphilia in the public mind. And with re-arrest rates for sexual offending under 10 percent in most studies, there is no foundation for the belief that the juvenile sex offenders pose a high danger to the community for future sexual predation. Based on criminal justice cohorts, more than nine out of ten times the arrest of a juvenile for a sex offense is a one-time event, even though the same offender may often be apprehended in the future for the same mix of nonsex offenses that is typical of other juvenile delinquents.

Identification of Sexually Dangerous Youth

But there must be some adolescents who later commit dangerous sex crimes, because all adult sex offenders pass through adolescence. Given the low general rate of sex-offender recidivism in the teen years, a priority concern should be identifying the characteristics that separate the dangerous few from the bulk of teen offenders who transition away from future involvement with recorded sex offenses.

At the outset, it is important to remember that we do not know what proportion of the population of chronic sex offenders have official records as juveniles. That is not a difficult issue to research, but the self-report studies reported to date do not provide any measure of the proportion of offenders with official records.

The relatively few prediction studies that use cohorts of identified juvenile offenders are not conclusive. Some status variables that predict higher recidivism in adult male offenders—youth and not being married—do not predict high rates of recidivism in populations that are all young and all unmarried such as juvenile sex offenders (see Liedecke and Marbibi, 2000, p. 34; Caldwell 2002). A male victim in prior offending is associated with higher re-arrest in some but not all studies. The one key predictor of higher levels of future recidivism in the study by Leidecke and Marbibi (2000) of the Texas prison release data is a history of multiple sex offenses (p. 33). Even then, the use of valid risk-prediction instruments on juvenile offenders coming out of prison generates high rates of false positives. The Texas study used a prediction instrument that captured all of the re-offenders in its high-risk category, but seventeen of the twenty-one members of this category for which four years of experience was available had no sex re-offending at that point, and the false positive rate at three years was 90 percent. Caldwell's (2002) analysis of ten studies produces no consistent pattern.

There are two reasons why the efforts to find subtypes of juvenile sex offenders have been unsuccessful to date. First, there has not been extensive research on the topic: "only a handful of studies have attempted to identify factors that distinguish juvenile sex offenders that persist in offending from those that do not." And second, in the small number of studies that have been published the "results are often conflicting" (Caldwell, 2002, p. 299).

Three Types of Adolescent Offender

The 15,000 children and adolescents under eighteen years of age arrested for sex crimes each year are a heterogeneous group in terms of their offense severity, their risk of future sexual misconduct, and their degree of psychological pathology. The great majority of youthful sex offenders are unlikely to re-offend, and are not suffering from extensive clinical disabilities. But the few thousand juveniles who are arrested, in contrast to the millions who commit sex crimes, are often involved in behavior that harms people, usually children and adolescents. The palpable harm caused by many juvenile sex offenders requires an official response. The low risk of future sexual misconduct and the low likelihood of serious sexual pathology argue against life-altering interventions and permanent classification in stigmatic categories as routine responses to adolescent sexual misconduct.

As a prelude to serious policy analysis, three types of juvenile sex offenders should be distinguished. The first can be called the "sexual status offender," those children and teens whose sexual behavior is only unlawful because their partners are under the age of consent. This is consensual conduct between age peers, unlawful because the law regards all sexual conduct by youth to be problematic. The percentage of all juvenile sex-offense arrests that fall into this category is not known.

The second and largest category of juvenile sex offenders are first offenders involved in abusive conduct, who are arrested either because they are much older than their partners or because force or coercion was used. The majority of all juvenile sex arrests fall into this category. While the severity of the offenses vary widely among this first-arrest group, the re-arrest rate for sex offenses is quite low.

The third type of juvenile sex offender is the repeat offender in abusive sexual conduct. The size of this group is relatively small, 4–8 percent of all juveniles arrested for sex crimes, but the number of juveniles in the category might still be as high as 1,000 per year. The repeat juvenile sexual offender has not been the subject of detailed studies based on representative samples from arrest populations, so the aggregate re-offending rate and the types of sexual offending are not yet known conclusively. It is probable that the repeat offender category is itself heterogeneous. Nothing can be said with confidence about the range of re-arrest probability because the group is so small in relation to first offenders that relatively high re-arrest rates could be present for the repeaters but not visible because of the much larger volume of very low-rate first offenders.

The overlap between repeat offending and sexual dangerousness is far from clear. Many adolescents with only one or no arrests for sex crimes may develop into sexually dangerous adults, just as many adolescents with repeat sex offenses might not. Still, the failure to focus on the varieties of repeat sexual offending among juvenile offenders is inexplicable. And the only appropriate strategy to study such groups is to locate them in representative samples of the youth population or of arrested juveniles.

Relying on the evidence presently available, a prediction of danger-ousness among any group of juvenile sex offenders is problematic. There are some adolescent offenders with clearly defined sexual pathologies, and some (but not all) of those offenders are at heightened risk of repetitive sex-ual offending. There are also sadistic and sexually violent youth who carry high dangers of future sexual violence whether or not they fit comfortably into clinical definitions of paraphilia. But the identification of high risk offenders in their teens is no easy task. Risk assessments in representative samples of offenders have produced few consistent predictors of height-ened risk, other than repetitive sexual misconduct in an offender's history. And the level of false positives in the limited prediction studies of criminal justice samples of juveniles has been quite high.

The practical problem for current policymaking is that the general risks associated with juvenile offenders are too low to justify extensive interven-tion, but the capacity to predict differential dangerousness in subpopula-tions is also quite limited. Since we cannot find the needle in the haystack, the choice is between overtreatment of large numbers of youth and failure to intervene with the dangerous few. Neither option is good public policy.

Chapter 4

The Emergence of Juvenile Sex-Offender Treatment

The number of juveniles arrested for sex offenses has remained stable over the past quarter century and there are no indications that the behaviors leading to arrests or the likelihood of repetition of sex crime has changed much in the past few decades. Indeed, there is reason to believe that officially reported juvenile sex offenses other than forcible rape are spread more evenly across the cities and suburbs of developed nations and are also less variable over time than many other types of youth criminality. But while the frequency and type of sex offending by the young has remained stable in the United States during the last two decades or so, attitudes concerning how to best respond to the problem have changed. This chapter documents and explores some of these changes.

Figure 4.1 shows the trends for the period 1975–2000 in arrests of persons under age eighteen for forcible rape and for other noncommercial sex offenses. The volume of arrests for both categories was relatively stable over the quarter century reported in the figure. The volume of forcible rape arrests never rose above 41 percent over its 1975 volume (in 1992) and then declined steadily to reach a twenty-five-year low in 2000, at 23 percent below the 1975 level. The arrest volume for the heterogeneous "other sex offense" category peaked in the same year as rape (1992) at 51 percent above its 1975 volume, and declined more slowly than rape in the late 1990s. By 1999 and 2000, the volume of arrests for this category equaled the 1975 volume. If the changing numbers of youth were factored in, the 1992 peak would have been substantially higher than in figure 4.1 (because the youth population had decreased) and the decline shown during the 1990s would have been more precipitous (because the adolescent population was increasing as arrest rates declined). But arrests in both these sex offense categories were much less volatile than in serious youth violence (Zimring, 1998, chap. 3). There are no indications of major change in juvenile sex crimes at any time in the last quarter of the twentieth century.

Juvenile Court Trends

There is no systematic national sample of juvenile court cases by charge available to assess trends in sex offenses over time, but existing data on trends in several states suggests a relatively flat pattern also for juvenile court cases where the most serious charge is a sex offense. The national juvenile court archives maintained by the National Center for Juvenile Justice contains records from juvenile courts in nineteen states of the distribution of delinquency cases by most serious charge. Because the number of courts participating in this survey varied from year to year, the volume of sex cases from the courts participating in the program is not as clear an indication of trends over time in juvenile court sex cases as is measuring trends in the proportion of reported cases each year during which a sex crime was the most serious charge (McCurley, Sickmund & Snyder, 2003). Figure 4.2 shows the proportion of all delinquency cases in the nineteen states that involved sex offenses as the most serious charge by year, from 1985 through 2000.

The sex cases varied from a high of 2.3 percent of total docketed charges (in 1985) to a low of 1.5 percent of all cases (in 1995 and 1996). The relative frequency of sex cases declined in the late 1980s and early 1990s because the volume of sex charges did not grow at anywhere near the rate of other types of delinquency charges. The percentage of total delinquency cases involving sex offenses then approximated its fifteen-year low through 1999, but rose to 2 percent for 2000, the last year in the series. For the last fifteen years of the twentieth century, however, the most noteworthy trend is that the juvenile court's sex docket did not increase as fast as other types of delinquency charges during periods of growth and did not decline as quickly as other charges in periods of decline. Stability, not decline, is the major theme in sex charge trends in representative jurisdictions after 1985.

But this stability in sex offense cases must be understood in the context of the broad enforcement discretion that produces the contrast discussed in the last chapter between multiple millions of criminal sexual acts by adolescents each year but only about 15,000 arrests, and even fewer cases pursued in the courts. What the data in figure 4.2 tell us is that there was no apparent change in the highly selective enforcement of the criminal law of adolescent sexuality in the nineteen states reporting to the juvenile court archive program. Because of the huge gap that has always existed

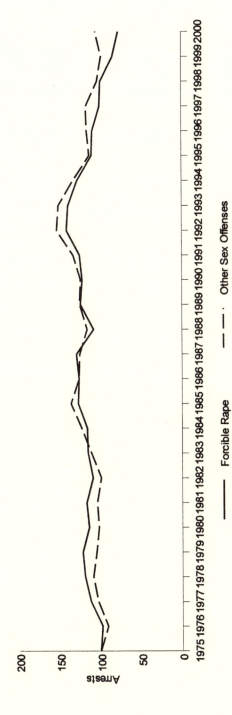

Figure 4.1. Trends in juvenile sex-offense arrests during 1975–2000 from the *Uniform Crime Reports*
Source: U.S. Department of Justice, Federal Bureau of Investigation, *Uniform Crime Reports* (1975–2000).

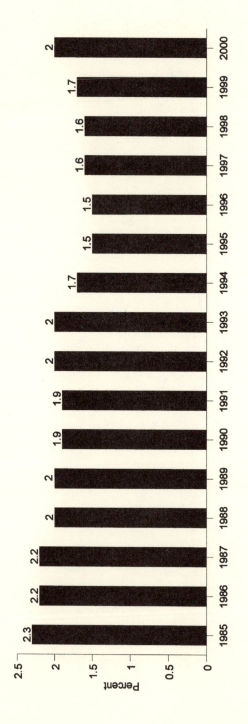

Figure 4.2. Proportion in nineteen states of juvenile court cases involving sex offenses during 1985–2000
Source: McCurley, Sickmund, & Snyder, 2003.

between prohibited and prosecuted adolescent sexual behavior, stable arrest and court charging rates are an indication of unchanging policy as much as an indication of the volume of offending over time.

For stable policy concerning police and court activity to have continued after 1985 is extraordinary in the face of (a) changing priorities in the punishment of adult offenders (chapter 2), (b) the intensification of child sex-offense reporting campaigns and the activity of victim advocacy, and (c) sexual-treatment program lobby efforts. The rising pressure during the last two decades of the twentieth century was toward more arrests and more prosecution.

Retention and Institutional Placement

No long-term data are available on rates of institutional placement for juvenile sex offenders, but a census of sex offenders in residential placement has reported every two years since 1997. Figure 4.3 shows trends in short-term detention and longer-term institutional placement for 1997, 1999, and 2001 as reported by the census to the National Center for Juvenile Justice. The reported volume of sex offenders in a wide variety of residential placements was 5,600 in 1997, with 85 percent of that total in longer-term commitments. Over the next two years, the number of offenders in long-term commitment rose 31 percent while the shorter detention category increased 44 percent. Between 1999 and the preliminary figures for 2001, both long- and short-term detention declined by about 10 percent. Over the four years as a whole, the growth in institutional population was just under 22 percent.

The Expansion of Juvenile Sex Offender Treatment

One response to the sexual misconduct of children and youth that seems to have changed rapidly over the last two decades of the twentieth century was the rise in institutional settings that define themselves as professional organizations dedicated to the treatment of juvenile sexual offenders. The growth of such programs is often illustrated by a finding in a report by the Safer Society program that "[w]hereas there were about 20 [juvenile sex offender] programs identified nationally in 1982, there are now (as of 1993) over 800 specialized treatment programs serving sexually abusive youth" (National Adolescent Perpetrator Network, 1993, p. 3). The 800 figure has continued to be used in the literature (Becker, 1998), but more recent sur-

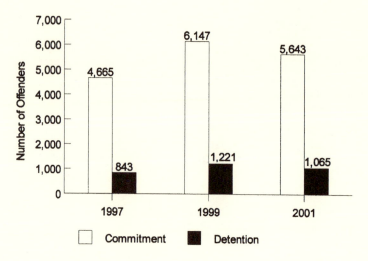

Figure 4.3. Sex offenders in residential detention and placement during 1997, 1999, and 2001

Source: Data reported to NCJJ Census by the U.S. Department of Commerce, Census Bureau.

veys have suggested the number of programs treating adolescents and children has declined over the past decade.

In 1996, 539 programs reported that they treated juveniles (Burton and Smith-Darden, 2000), and a survey conducted in the year 2000 reported only 357 programs with adolescent or child subjects (Burton and Smith-Darden, 2001). The decline in programs between 1993 and 1996 did not involve any significant change in reporting and classification, so the 1996 estimate of 539 should be comparable to the earlier 800 estimate. The year 2000 survey, however, would only count a program with different types of clients in one category, so the further drop in program numbers after 1996 may be an artifact of the new classification system (Burton and Smith-Darden, 2001). Still, whether the growth in programs was twentyfold or tenfold, dramatic real growth in formal treatment for juvenile sex offenders occurred after 1980. This expansion of programs and treatment staff created a new constituency in the legal response to juvenile sex misconduct.

There is unfortunately no consistent information on the number of clients treated in the several surveys published in the 1980s and 1990s, but the survey by Burton and Smith-Darden (2000) did include reports from programs on the number of subjects treated during calendar year 1998. This survey is the best data available on the extent to which sex treatment is used in juvenile justice.

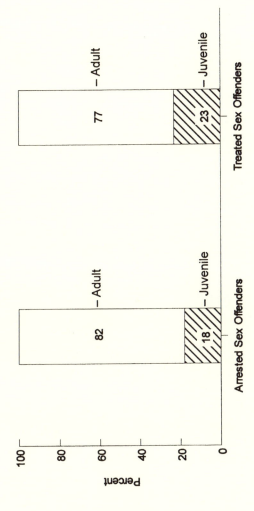

Figure 4.4. Percentage distribution between adults and juveniles for sex offenders arrested and sex offenders in treatment

Sources: U.S. Department of Justice, 2000; Burton & Smith-Darden, 2001.

Figure 4.4 compares the breakdown into adult and juvenile categories of sex offenders who receive treatment with persons arrested for sex crimes. Children and adolescents are modestly overrepresented in the treatment population when compared to their share of sex offense arrests, comprising 23 percent of the treatment group but 18 percent of total arrests for rape and other noncommercial sex offenses. The rate of treatment per 100 sex offense arrests is 36 percent higher for juveniles than for adults.

The 6,422 children and adolescents treated by respondent programs in 1998 represent about 40 percent of the number of juveniles arrested for sex offenses in the United States, if we guess that 3.8 percent of the treated youth were from the 3.8 percent of programs located in Canadian provinces. Sixty percent of the children and adolescents treated were seen by community-based programs, while 40 percent were assigned to residential programs. The survey does not indicate what proportion of the 2,558 youth treated in residential programs are in locked facilities, but 26 percent of all the residential programs were listed as "juvenile corrections," and an additional 16 percent were categorized as hospital based or court sponsored (Burton and Smith-Darden, 2001, p. 8).

The National Adolescent Perpetrator Network and Its Report

This chapter's focus is on the principles and practice of a national network of juvenile sex-treatment professionals that has been active and influential since the late 1980s. This vocal and well-organized network of treatment units for juvenile sex offenders is not a standard group of mental health professionals by any means. It is instead a hybrid group combining elements of several different groups that were active in the United States during the 1980s and 1990s. Part mental health treatment group, part victim advocacy organization, part social movement to take power away from judges and police in the name of therapeutic control of juvenile sex offenders, the individuals and organizations that coalesced to form the National Adolescent Perpetrator Network represent an offense-specific treatment movement without precedent in American juvenile justice.

The 105-page report of the National Adolescent Perpetrator Network that was published in 1993 demands sustained attention for three reasons. First, this group has been the most visible body concerned with juvenile sex offenders as a treatment specialty. Subgroups associated with the report by the network in 1993 have published plans for a variety of states (see National Adolescent Perpetrator Network, 1993, pp. 109–110), and the main report that is the focus of this chapter was published in the *Juvenile Judge's*

Journal; this report was the longest publication devoted to sex offenders in the literature of juvenile justice for at least half a century. Second, the program for juvenile justice involvement in sex-offender cases advocated by this group is both ambitious and novel. It prescribes regimes of compulsory prosecution and extraordinary extensions of power over adolescent offenders. For juvenile sex offenders, it would change most of the priorities and tactics of the juvenile court from traditional practice, as the chapter will show.

The third reason the 1993 document requires sustained attention is that it has not been subjected to detailed and critical scrutiny in all the years that it has been the most visible landmark in the theory and practice of juvenile sex-offender treatment in the United States. This report of the National Task Force on Juvenile Sexual Offending teaches important lessons about the conflicts and dangers produced when punitive and treatment agendas are mixed. It draws attention to many of the hard questions encountered when choosing strategies to respond to sexual offending by children and adolescents. And it shows conclusively the danger of any current program advocacy that ignores the lessons learned during the first hundred years of juvenile courts. The bulk of this chapter will review the final Task Force report as a profile of one organized branch of the juvenile sex-offender treatment community and as a case study of the mixture of punitive and therapeutic agendas. My review of the approach to juvenile offenders advocated by the Task Force will serve as a bridge between the first section of this book—a profile of current practice—and the last three chapters that look toward reforms in the legal and institutional responses to juvenile sexual offenders.

The National Adolescent Perpetrator Network profiled in this chapter is not the only organized professional group dedicated to the treatment of sex offenders. There is also an Association of Sex Treatment Professionals with its own set of principles and agenda concerning the treatment of juveniles that is in many respects different from the positions taken by the National Task Force. So it should not be assumed that the National Task Force report speaks for all of those involved in adolescent offender treatment efforts. Indeed, it is possible that a professional in the field might favor some version of sex counseling and treatment for juvenile offenders that the National Task Force would totally reject. But judging from the lack of critical reaction to the 1993 report and the ways in which it is emulated in many state plans, the Task Force report should be accorded some degree of authority as a professional view of appropriate responses to juvenile sex offenders.

The Methods and Assumptions of the Sex Offender Task Force

The 1993 revised report by the National Task Force is not shy about its critique of prior practices and assumptions. The report begins with the following statement:

> Historically, juveniles involved in sexually offending behaviors were not held accountable for the victim impact or the criminal nature of these acts. Sexual behaviors which were clearly exploitative and criminal were often dismissed as "adolescent adjustment reactions," a manifestation of emotional disturbance, or defined as "experimentation." Even those youth whose cases were brought to court often were met with a "boys will be boys" attitude, or the charges were reduced to nonsexual charges before being filed. It has only been since the mid- to late-1970s that these practices have been scrutinized and special intervention has been developed for sexually abusive youth. (National Adolescent Perpetrator Network, 1993, p. 5)

POLICY BY ASSUMPTION. Facing many questions about matters for which scientific data are missing, the Task Force report makes use of factual assumptions that are widely shared among its members as the foundation for basing policy recommendations. "Within this document, statements labeled 'Assumptions' represented the basic underlying principles which are the foundation of current thinking and practice in the field. These assumptions reflect at least 90% agreement within the Task Force" (National Adolescent Perpetrator Network, 1993, p. 7). The 1993 report is based on no fewer than 387 assumptions about adolescent behavior, appropriate justice system responses, dangerousness, and the impact of various interventions on the long-term development and life opportunities of juvenile offenders. I think that substituting assumptions for assertions of factual evidence can be regarded as "postmodern" in its implicit judgment that unambiguous empirical evidence cannot be available and in the conclusion that shared attitudes and beliefs can serve just as well for making policy decisions and for evaluating competing claims about what might be good for young people. (Michael Tonry of the Cambridge Institute of Criminology first proposed this interpretation.)

But even if one is not a fan of the postmodern, reading a policy-oriented position paper that announces that it is based on 387 unproven assumptions is a refreshing change from many policy arguments that announce they are based on evidence but then turn out to depend on unadvertised and unproven assumptions. There is an element of truth-in-advertising to the Task Force's willingness to make policy-by-assumption into the featured method of its analysis. But there are also three obvious defects in the way the Task Force uses assumptions about factual reality that make much of its analysis unreliable. The first problem is that widely shared assumptions are not the functional equivalent of an empirical proof, and no amount of wishful thinking can make agreed-on assumptions into the hard currency of empirical knowledge. Yet giving the assumptions and the procedures that produce them the center stage in this report does seem to imply that agreement among clinicians is a sufficient empirical foundation for legal policies, even when factual evidence is sparse or nonexistent.

A second problem with the 387 assumptions that drive the 1993 National Task Force on Juvenile Sexual Offending is the rather narrow band of nonmedical clinical sex-program personnel who passed judgment on the assumptions in the report. The Task Force describes the network that produced the effort as a "multidisciplinary group of individuals who have been actively networking and sharing ideas since 1983" (National Adolescent Perpetrator Network, 1993, p. 5). Since the only basis for trusting the shared beliefs that drive policy choices is the broad agreement between consulted professionals, a diverse group of experts with different interests and different types of expertise would be an important criterion for trust. But almost all the members of the Task Force were practitioners active in treatment rather than researchers, and this generates a natural bias toward lower standards of evidence for policies and practice (Tarvis, 2003). The network that produces the 387 assumptions in the 1993 report is a self-selected group of professionals enthusiastic about sex-offender treatment and invested in the current beliefs and practices of such treatment. Skeptics, and those with professional status in program evaluation and policy analysis, are not a prominent part of the polity whose shared opinions came to represent facts in this report.

And skeptics are not the only missing persons in this Task Force's interdisciplinary assemblage. The medical profession and medically trained personnel are also notably absent. There were no M.D.'s among the twenty-five "participating" Task Force members and only one M.D. was listed as an "advisory member." This resulted in an evident inattention to medical perspectives. The detailed approach to sexual disorders in the *Diagnostic and Statistical Manual* of the American Psychiatric Association is *nowhere* referred to in the body or references of the Task Force report, despite its use of medical terms and diagnoses (paraphilia, pedophilia, fetish, and so on) and despite some sharp differences between psychiatric diagnostic criteria and the clinical predictions of future behavior that motivate the Task Force's recommendations.

The legal profession is also not well represented, and this underrepresentation also may have led to problematic assumptions. Only one attorney, a former prosecutor, was a member of the participating Task Force. Among the problematic assumptions underlying the Task Force's jurisprudence of treatment is that making incarceration a consequence of unfavorable treatment recommendations (p. 53) would not compromise the "informed consent" the Task Force would require from juveniles regarding polygraphs (p. 85), waiver of all confidentiality claims (p. 121), and phalometric assessments (p. 81). The Task Force recommends the waiver of any expectation of confidentiality to disclosures during therapy of past as well as planned acts, but the distinction between past and planned conduct is never discussed, nor is the combination of a compulsory polygraph in treatment with complete absence of confidentiality ever addressed as a potential policy problem.

Also absent among the Task Force members are experts on the history and functions of juvenile justice. Nowhere is the long history of the American juvenile court in treating the sexually threatening behavior of mostly female status offenders mentioned in the Task Force report, nor are the precursors to sex-offender treatments in earlier juvenile court clinics and institutions mentioned. Despite recommending major changes in the caseloads and operations of juvenile courts, the report displays little knowledge of the consequences of shifts in policy on the various components of the juvenile justice system.

The third major problem with the use by the Task Force of shared assumptions rather than facts is that the report does not acknowledge the tentativeness of its evidence nor display an awareness of the vulnerability of its premises to disproof. Tentativeness and humility are appropriate when fundamental policy proposals are based only on the shared beliefs of practitioners. But the 1993 report is never tentative when most of its members agree on an assumption. Only when consensus is absent does the Task Force hesitate to come to firm conclusions. When most of the sex therapists at the meeting agree, their opinions are regarded as a solid factual foundation for radical changes in legal policy.

This chapter provides a selective introduction into the substance of the 1993 Task Force recommendations and the worldview that informs them. The next section briefly outlines the ways in which the Task Force would like to change the system that currently exists to respond to criminal sexual misconduct by children and adolescents under eighteen. I follow this summary with a more detailed discussion of several key assumptions the Task Force has made about the character of adolescent sexual misconduct and its treatment, and mention also some crucially important questions that the report does not address. I then discuss the objectives and tactics of sex-offender treatment proposed by the Task Force report. The concluding part of my tour through the report places it in historical context and compares the ideology it reflects with other theories of state response to juvenile misconduct.

A New Order

The system advocated by the 1993 Task Force is one in which all sexual conduct committed by children and youths that is illegal under current standards (or would be considered illegal if the child committing it had been older) would be referred to juvenile courts by social service agencies, child custodians, educators, and police. All offending children and youth would be screened by sex-offender therapists and coerced into treatment if a therapist concluded that treatment was clinically necessary. Diversion by police and court personnel would be discouraged or forbidden, and reporting by other professionals of any illegal sex incidents would be required by law. Treatment would be combined with punishment (this encourages "accountability") and would continue as long as was thought necessary. The Task Force report also advocates long-term registration and tracking of all juvenile offenders, and toward this end would allow for revision of the current legal protection of juveniles (Assumption 213, p. 56) without any stated limit.

In the Task Force's view, both prosecution and punishment are in the interests of the juvenile offender, but any conflict between the offender's interests and community safety should in all cases be resolved in favor of community safety because "the community is the client" in this branch of the healing professions (Assumption 1, p. 12). (How that policy might ever permit the release of subjects from restraint or treatment is not addressed.)

The Task Force is explicit in its wish to undermine any discretion on the part of teachers, social workers, or the police not to report the commission of sex offenses or to divert offenders away from the juvenile justice system. Prosecution is explicitly called for in all cases, though no formal controls on discretion are proposed for prosecutors or juvenile court judges. I discuss the differences between these policies urged by the Task Force and the standard policies and practices of modern juvenile justice after a review of some of the major assumptions that animate the report.

Some Critical Assumptions

The 1993 Task Force report neither describes nor judges the current policies or practices of juvenile courts in nonsexual delinquency cases in the United States. Instead, it is asserted that "sexually abusive youth require a specialized response from the justice system which is different from other delinquent populations" (National Adolescent Perpetrator Network, 1993, 86). But the Task Force never describes what it considers the proper response to other delinquent youth or the reasons for believing that sex offenders are different from other young offenders. A reader is left to sift through the details of the report's description of juvenile sex offenders for indications of what it considers their special nature and special needs to be. Does the Task Force think that children and juveniles who fall into its sex offender categories are sexual deviants?

The problem with this approach is the way in which the Task Force defines its population at risk. The key term in the report is "sexually abusive behavior." Any young person who commits a "sexually abusive act," we are told, is *ipso facto* different from other delinquent offenders. But again we ask whether the young person who commits a "sexually abusive act" is thought of by the Task Force as a sexual deviant. There is no estimate *anywhere* in the report of the extent to which sexual abuse and any recognized forms of mental or emotional illness overlap. Instead, the reader is told that "[t[he crime of sexual abuse is a *legal* construct based on societal values and norms" (p. 6, italics added). Later in its discussion, the report acknowledges that "[w]e are often unprepared to substantiate what is 'normal' and what is 'deviant' sexual behavior in juveniles" (pp. 6–7, inner quotation marks in original). But rather than attempting to discriminate between normal and deviant behavior, the report retreats to a standard that defines all illegal behaviors as abusive, including that by children otherwise too young for their acts to qualify as illegal, so long as the same sexual conduct is illegal if committed by older juveniles. "Intervention with sexually abusive youth should not be based on the value judgments of individuals but on the legal constructs of this society" (p. 7).

But creating a legal standard of that sort produces two unsolvable problems for this Task Force on juvenile sex offenders. In the first place, there is absolutely no clinical evidence of deviance that can be inferred from law violation alone. Indeed, with all the statutory age-of-consent limits imposed on consensual youngsters by the criminal laws concerning indecent liberties and statutory rape, there is no logical reason to support an inference of sexual abuse from the violation of a criminal standard. Petting and intercourse involving fifteen-year-olds is felonious in most states. It is only "sexually abusive behavior" because the Task Force defines it as such.

Yet if illegal sexual conduct has no necessary relationship to sexual deviance or emotional maladjustment, what is there that necessitates treatment of every sexual act by children and teens that violates the criminal law? If therapists should treat every person who commits a sex-law violation in the United States, why shouldn't they also treat all burglars (who abuse property rights and scare homeowners) and car thieves? So the first problem with regarding any violation of criminal law as a sufficient condition for concluding the presence of sexual abuse and instituting its treatment is that there is no necessary connection between law violation and the existence of any sexual disorder that should require treatment.

The second problem with letting law violation define the sexual abuse standard is that there is no reason to suppose that sex-law violators are any different from shoplifters, adolescents who commit aggravated assault, or drug-law violators. If one conclusively defines any youth who violates a criminal statue dealing with drugs, alcohol, or tobacco as a "substance abuser," and if the law required the compulsory reporting of all illegal drug and alcohol use and referral to a treatment network, the result would be a new control apparatus that would be expected to deal with millions of youthful abusers. But would they all really need treatment? For what? In this light, it is conspicuous that nowhere in the 120 pages of its 1993 report does the Task Force clearly state the reason why all sex-law violators need treatment.

The only way to legitimate a special treatment rationale for sex offenders as opposed to kids who drink alcohol and smoke marijuana is to focus on the special harm of sex crime or the special dangers of juveniles who commit such offenses. Both of these approaches are present in the rhetoric of the Task Force report, but both justifications are also undermined by the Task Force's insistence that all sex-law violations need to be treated and punished. Chapter 3 suggested that many if not most of the acts that generate juvenile sex-offense arrests under the current system do have clear victims, either because some force or coercion was used or because they involved children much younger than the arrested participant. But the major reason for this high percentage of true victim crimes is not the standards in criminal law but rather the extensive discretionary work by police and court personnel who screen for the commission of real harm. But this is the very same discretion rejected by the Task Force in favor of compulsory prosecution. Without extensive screening it is probably the case that a clear majority of unlawful sexual contacts involving teenagers lack a "victim."

A policy of compulsory reporting, arrest, and prosecution also undermines any argument that juvenile sex offenders are an especially dangerous class of juvenile delinquents. Certainly the term "sex abusers" sounds dangerous, but its use as a way of defining all sex-law violators robs the term of any real dangerousness. The Task Force explicitly regards juveniles who make obscene phone calls and sexually harassing announcements as "serious components the continuum of sexually abusive behaviors" (p. 7). No data are presented on the actuarial experience of these or any other broad sample of juvenile sex defendants. The data reviewed in chapter 3 on arrest samples of juvenile sex offenders show low sexual re-offending rates combined with higher levels of general delinquency. This suggests great continuity between current sex offenders and other delinquents rather than any special dangerousness of the sex offender. Adding millions of sexual-status offenders into the mix, as the Task Force recommends, would make sex offenders less dangerous than other delinquents.

Among the key implicit assumptions of the Task Force report are that all youth who violate sex laws "require a specialized offense specific treatment" (Assumption 112, p. 35), that it is dangerous to release juvenile sex offenders without "offense specific treatment options" (Assumption 120, p. 36), and that "[d]irect participation in the prosecution process is helpful to the offender" (p. 19). The report also asserts without explanation that "[p]rosecution should be pursued in any incident which involves a sexual crime where sufficient evidence supports a case" (Assumption 35, p. 19). "Legal accountability is important for juveniles in developing self responsibility" (p. 19). And "[t]he legal process is an integral part of the corrective process" (p. 19).

The Adversarial Therapist

Another critical assumption of the 1993 Task Force is that an adversarial relationship between a therapist and an adolescent offender is appropriate and effective. The treatment process as described by the Task Force is certainly one designed to ensure that such an adversarial relationship exists. The therapist's real client is said to be the community (Assumption 1, p. 12) and the therapist's principle goal is sex crime prevention (Assumption 118, p. 36). Her tools include polygraphy, confrontation, and no obligation of confidentiality to the client. All of this is assumed to be in the client's best interests because it will help him stay out of future trouble.

The therapist's adversarial relationship toward adolescent sex offenders is never explicitly explained but emanates from a series of priorities (disclosure, polygraphs, and so forth). Yet there are powerful indications in the text of the 1993 report that adolescent offenders are regarded as enemies by the therapists. One particularly poignant indication of this hostility to teen sex offenders is found by comparing the Task Force's standards relating to very young children entering sex therapy with its policy toward adolescents. First, Assumption 252 states that "[s]ince it is not yet possible to know which children who exhibit sexually abusive behavior may cease these behaviors either spontaneously or as a result of treatment and which are most at risk to continue abusive behaviors over time, early interventions should label the behavior without labeling the child" (p. 66). This can be recognized as a proper goal for therapeutic intervention whether or not accurate predictions can be made about a child's later risk. Indeed, it is part of the process of identifying with the child while trying to eliminate troubling behavior, a standard therapeutic aim. As such, doesn't the Task Force seek to accomplish the same with all juvenile sex offenders?

No, it does not. There is nothing equivalent in the Task Force to Assumption 252 for children over ten years old. Yet the difficulty in predicting future sexual offending with or without treatment interventions is notorious among adolescents, as we saw in chapter 3. It is also not the real point of the treatment standard underlying Assumption 252. Therapists are admonished in this report to "label the behavior without labeling the child" when treating very young children only in contrast to the blaming, the stigmatization, and the permanent labeling that are the encouraged standard practice with offenders over age eleven. The group that prepared this report called itself the National Adolescent Perpetrator Network, which by its name alone indicates its intent to label both offenders and their offending behaviors. In this light it is clear that the Task Force needed to come up with contrasting therapeutic strategies concerning those children young enough to avoid the sting of the Network.

Another standard for treatment of sexual misconduct on the part of young children is Assumption 253, which reminds therapists that "specialized treatment for sexually abusive behavior in childhood must be respectful of children's developmental needs and address developmental deficits" (p. 66). I do not underscore this assumption because I find it surprising or problematic. Nothing could be less surprising than a reminder for therapists to consider a patient's developmental needs during periods of rapid and significant physical and emotional development.

But is there a period of more rapid, profound, and confusing sexual development than puberty and adolescence? A reader of the 1993 report nevertheless will search in vain for a parallel admonition that therapists who hold themselves out as experts on the treatment of adolescents must be respectful of adolescents developmental needs and address developmental deficits associated with adolescence. It turns out that none of the solicitous attention to development that is usual in therapeutic relationships with children and adolescents is advocated by the Task Force. Instead, adolescent developmental needs are a casualty of the war the Task Force seems to declare on teen offenders.

Some Questions Not Asked

With a methodology that substitutes assumptions for factfinding, there is no obvious reason why the 1993 Task Force should have ignored important issues relating to juvenile sex offenders. But there are three areas of fundamental importance unexplored by the 1993 report. The first issue is the developmental context of adolescent sexual offending and the extent to which transient developmental needs and developmental deficits are the proximate causes of sexual offenses during adolescence.

The first paragraph of the 1993 report tells readers that assumptions in prior eras that offending was part of "adolescent adjustment reactions" or "experimentation" were policy errors. But that marks the last examination of male adolescent sexual conduct in developmental context in the report! There is no attempt to estimate the proportion or rate of offenses that are part of a transitory or transitional status or that are importantly linked to the offenders inability to initiate peer sexual relations because of developmental deficits. The emphasis in treatment discussions on sex education suggests that transitional or deficit-based offending is an important element (see National Adolescent Perpetrator Network, 1993, sections 18 and 20), but the introduction to the report seems to assume that because adolescent offenders can be blamed for their criminal acts, the etiology of such offenses is not important. So the types of offenses that might be transitional and the proportion of teen offenses and arrests that have developmental links are not addressed in a report that focuses on the adolescent offender.

The second issue not addressed in the Task Force report is the extent to which adolescent sexual offending is the result of clinically significant forms of sexual deviance. In its introduction, the Task Force suggests this might be a particular problem with a youth population for developmental reasons ("we are often unprepared to substantiate what is 'normal' and what is 'deviant' sexual behavior in juveniles [p. 7]). But having once identified the issue, the report never again addresses it. The proportion of "paraphilic" behaviors in the total incidence of juvenile sex crime could be 5 percent, 20 percent, or 50 percent, but the question is not considered. Having created an aggregate category of abuse that is defined only on a legal basis, the analysis never attempts to sort out the impact of any clinical conditions on the problem behavior.

Yet despite the fact that the incidence and prevalence of paraphilia in juvenile sex offending is never addressed, the presence of clinically significant conditions is assumed in some of the Task Force's discussion of treatment. The first principle announced in the report's discussion of the theory of treatment is "that deviant arousal patterns develop in response to victimization or by the results of learned behavior" (p. 46), and four other theoretical premises are also focused on deviant behavior (pp. 46–47). But this assertion is made without any evidence put forth that deviant arousal is a significant part of juvenile offending. The report announces that some juvenile sexual offenders present with concurrent diagnoses *in addition to the identified paraphilia* (Assumption 268, p. 69). But again there is no evidence concerning or even assumptions made about the role of paraphilia in juvenile sexual offending. What diagnoses are associated with which types of juvenile sexual crime? What is the extent of the overlap? The report does assume that all juvenile offenders need treatment, but it never tells us for what. The sole presenting symptom for juvenile sex-offender treatment is unlawful behavior.

The third major set of concerns not addressed in the Task Force report are the similarities and differences between juvenile and adult sex offenders. What features distinguish fifteen-year-old boys arrested for sexual abuse of eight-year-old girls from forty-two-year-old men arrested on the same charges? Are the adults more often diagnosable with a paraphilia? Does such behavior in the midteens present the same risk of reoccurrence as for adult offenders? We shall see in chapter 7 that the extent to which adolescent offenders fit the predominant assumptions about adult offenders is a critical matter for public policy regarding notification and registration systems. But there is no systematic comparison of offense patterns in different developmental stages in the Task Force report.

The failure to address the developmental aspects of juvenile offending, or the relationship or lack of relationship between sexual deviance and sexual offending in youth, or the contrast or similarities between juvenile and adult sex offending leave this single-purpose network dedicated to the treatment of juvenile offenders without a clear rationale guiding its specialized focus. In sum, the Task Force on juvenile sexual offending has created a structure of specialized treatment without providing any foundation of basic reasons for the separate diagnosis or treatment of the juvenile offender.

New Frontiers of Sexual Deviance

There are two places in the Task Force's definition of terms where language is used in ways that are symptomatic of significant problems of judgment and perspective. The first, and lesser, problem concerns a list of clinical terms, most of them specific sexual disorders, that is defined for laypersons and policymakers early in the report. Sandwiched between "floraphilia" (the sexual attraction to plants) and "pedophilia" (the sexual interest in young children), under the heading of "behaviors associated with an individual's sexual arousal," the reader is presented with the term "hebophilia," defined as the "sexual interest in adolescents" (National Adolescent Perpetrator Network, 1993, p. 11). Nowhere in the report is this term used in the analysis of juvenile sex offenders or their treatment. But the clear implication of its inclusion in the list is that sexual attraction to or focus on adolescents is a problematic condition, a paraphilia to be diagnosed and combated in treatment. What makes this implication preposterous is the report's context, an analysis of the sexual tastes and conduct of children and adolescents. The sexual focus on adolescents by adolescents would seem to be both normal and normative. Why would a document concerned with this population use a term like "hebophilia" in such a way as to give it a clinical connotation?

The second definitional misstep in the report is a more frightening abuse of language and clinical knowledge. Just as law violation becomes sexual abuse by linguistic convention in the Task Force report, an odd set of stipulative definitions provides an extraordinary expansion of the usual meanings of language in relation to child molestation. The Task Force defines "molestation" as "to make annoying sexual advances toward; to use sexually without consent," and defines "child molestation" as "molestation of a juvenile" (p. 10). The report also defines "juvenile" as "any person less than 18 years of age" (p. 8). This Task Force has thereby decided that anybody with a history of making annoying sexual advances to seventeen-year-old girls is a child molester.

There are a number of problems with grouping annoying sexual advances toward seventeen-year-old girls and vaginal penetration of six-year-olds under the same category—namely, "child molestation." It mixes harmful behavior with obnoxious behavior, attempts to request consensual sex between peers with exploitative sex, unlawful behavior with allowed behavior. It degrades a legal and moral classification, and it is pointless. When this type of Orwellian misuse of language is made explicit by definition in the official report of an association of sex treatment professionals, it imperils the credibility of the group.

By the standards of the National Task Force on Juvenile Sexual Offending, a majority of American men and boys have committed multiple acts of child molestation by the time they reach their twenty-first birthdays. More than half of all males will have had sexual relations with females under eighteen, and many more will have made "annoying sexual advances" toward girls under 18. This aggregation of such behavior into a single category of "child molestation" is an extraordinary abuse for an organization of therapists. That such a gross misdefinition did not draw any critical commentary for a decade after its publication is also a reason for worry.

The Ends and Means of Juvenile Sex-Offender Treatments

What types of treatment are prescribed for juvenile sex offenders and what methods are used by therapists in their treatment plans? There is no single core treatment approach recommended by the 1993 Task Force, and no mention of either a single treatment method or combination of methods shown to reduce sexual re-offending by juvenile offenders. The report indicates that the topics to be covered in a treatment program are quite diverse.

The Task Force report provides a list of no fewer than thirty-four different value and behavior topics that should be the subject of juvenile sex-offender treatment, and also cautions that even this should be regarded as a "partial list" of the elements of treatment. Appendix B to this book provides a complete list of these treatment targets, a collection of issues that range from self-esteem and substance abuse to long-term management of sexually deviant impulses. The majority of issues listed as treatment targets are topics of concern to all adolescents—things like sexual development and identity, cultural influences on sex-role stereotyping, assertiveness training, and education; at least twenty-three of the thirty-four topics on the Task Force list represent matters of such universal concerns in adolescence (see appendix B). Six other topics identified for treatment emphasis seem to be issues of special concern for teens at high risk of delinquency but are not specific to sex: accountability for abusive behavior, high-risk decision-making, and the development of empathy for victims. Yet these are priority concerns for all delinquents. Five of the thirty-four target topics concern sex offending specifically: concerns with cycles of abuse, the offender's history of sex-offending behavior, and the ability to be pleased by nonexploitative sexual relationships are the three topics from this list of relevance to juvenile sex offenders of all kinds. The other two special sex-offender concerns—deviant fantasizing and arousal and the long-term management of deviant impulses—presumably arise only when substantial evidence of sexual deviance is present. Since the Task Force considers all unlawful sexuality to be abusive, good evidence of deviance will only be present in a small minority of cases (see chapter 3).

Which treatment methods are linked with which treatment topics is not discussed in the Task Force report. Presumably most of the educational materials on dating, assertiveness training, family dysfunction, and employment skills do not require polygraph examinations or adversarial confrontation. So a good deal of garden-variety counseling and information is mixed in with the monitoring, confrontation, and control techniques that focus on the offender's previous sex offenses and current sexual desires. How this mix of different methods should be maintained and its effect on the relationship between therapist and patient is not addressed in the Task Force report.

ABUSE OR DEVIANCE? There is one obvious problem with the 1993 Task Force list of topics for sex treatment. The report does not distinguish between sexual abuse (its primary topic) and sexual deviancy. Yet treating an entire population for problems and impulses that only some of them have is more than inefficient; it is potentially catastrophic and cruelly confusing to the target of treatment. If the accurate diagnosis of many forms of deviance in the early years of adolescence is as difficult as the medical profession believes (see DSM IV, 302.2C), false-positive labeling is a genuine problem that must be confronted by conscientious professionals. Sexual abuse as defined by this Task Force should never be equated with sexual deviance.

The methods used to monitor and inform the targets of juvenile sex-offender treatment vary widely. Some juvenile offenders are confined in secure institutional settings, some in group homes, while most are supervised in the community. Some are interrogated with polygraphs (168 programs indicate some use of this device) (National Adolescent Perpetrator Network, 1993, p. 80), and many are monitored in school and work situations. Most of the talking therapies mentioned in the 1993 report are versions of guided group interaction involving peers or therapist-led groups or individual sessions. We are not told what proportion of sex offenders are referred to any forms of treatment, or which types of intervention are most common, or how long treatments last, or how they end. And there is no evidence of any successful impact of interventions on future behavior. It is known that subjects who complete treatment often do better afterward than those who drop out of treatment (Becker, 1988). But the high compliance group that completes treatment is self-selected and differs from noncompleters in many ways. We do not know whether treatment is associated with reduced youth sex-offender recidivism from this type of comparison for the same reason that the lower heart-attack risks of women who self-selected to take hormone supplements was famously bad evidence that the supplements aided heart health. (It turned out that the self-selected hormone seekers were a very health-conscious group; it also turned out that controlled experiments showed no heart benefits of the treatment.)

PROSECUTION AS TREATMENT. Among the modalities of sex-offender therapy identified in the 1993 report of the Task Force, one new claim is worth special notice. Because what it calls "accountability" is a goal of treatment, the prosecution and punishment of sex offenders in court is claimed to be itself therapeutic: "Legal accountability is important for juveniles in developing self-responsibility. . . . Direct participation in the prosecution process is helpful to the offender" (National Adolescent Perpetrator Network, 1993, p. 19). This notion lends important support to the Task Force's call for nondiscretionary reporting and police arrest policy. But no data is provided to indicate that accountability has positive behavioral effects. There is also no awareness in the Task Force report of the inconsistency of this assumption with the predictions of labeling theory, a famous if not conclusively demonstrated tenet of modern sociological theory about delinquency (Laub, 2002).

Even though the claim is made by the Task Force that prosecution is beneficial for the juvenile offender, this does not mean that it sees making decisions about prosecution as an explicit way to ensure the offender's interests or wishes are taken seriously. The Task Force identifies no fewer than thirteen "purposes of prosecution" that it hopes will inform the legal process, yet none of the these are designed to encourage, support, or validate the offender (p. 19). Punishment, control-oriented treatment, victims' rights, and creation of a permanent record of the offender's wrongdoing are the listed motives of prosecution (p. 19), but these are asserted to be in the interests of the offender only because (it is assumed) these processes will reduce his risk as a future law violator.

But what does this have to do with sex-offender treatment? Why is a list of thirteen reasons to prosecute juvenile sex violators given prominent attention in a manual on treatment of offenders that is compiled by a group of clinicians? And when did these therapists become expert in the operation of law enforcement and juvenile justice agencies?

The willingness of treatment staff to participate in punishment, in labeling, and in the denunciation of treatment subjects is a remarkable part of the 1993 Task Force's version of sex-offender therapy. To paraphrase the report, the treatment goal for adolescents is apparently to "label the behavior *and* the adolescent." A conflict between the goals of treatment for offenders on the one hand and social control responsibilities on the other has been noted in other contexts, such as probation and parole. But those mixed treatment and control agents are usually state employees who officially represent the interests of social control. Here, those so enthusiastic for social control are to be found in the ranks of treatment professionals, and often in the private sector. Indeed, the report begins with a harsh critique of the permissiveness of the traditional juvenile court in the era of "adolescent adjustment reaction" (p. 5). There may be no conflict with the interests and goals of treatment because there is no identification with the adolescent offenders who are the targets of such treatment.

TREATMENT AND POWER. Not only does the treatment profession take a hard line on juvenile sex offenders, it also seeks to assume authority concerning legal and law enforcement decisions about whether acts get reported to the police or state agencies, about police discretion to bring charges, and about standards for prosecution. The values and preferences of sex-treatment staff become in this report the animating principles of the entire state response to juvenile sex misconduct. In that sense, the Task Force program is the triumph of the therapeutic state.

But this adamant legalism represents a peculiar version of the therapeutic state. The central standards of the Task Force that sex therapy seeks to enforce are not rooted in psychology nor in any behavioral science. This is therapy in the service of legal standards. Sex abuse is whatever the law prohibits. What is being treated is not a deviation from clinical standards but a deviation from legal standards. It is not that police, judges, and prosecutors have reoriented their approaches to become agents of clinical understanding of sexual development. That may have been the intention of earlier juvenile justice policies, but the Task Force believes this to have been misguided. So it is, instead, a system in which the therapeutic community has appointed itself the sheriff, taking over authority previously residing in judges and police and doing so in the unquestioning service of the legal standards governing what is permitted and what forbidden in adolescent sex.

IDEOLOGY AND PRACTICE. Does the Task Force report represent the assumptions and intentions of therapists working in more than 500 programs across the United States? There are several reasons to suspect that the operating ideology of those therapists engaged in the practice of counseling and supervising adolescent subjects might vary widely (and tend to be less hostile and legalistic) than the rhetoric in the 1993 Task Force report. This is not a report that has any official standing, nor is it a series of recommendations that went through the watering-down of controversial statements by broadly based committees and interest groups. It was instead written by volunteers (who tend to be activists) and vetted through an activist task force of volunteer members.

The document also may reflect the incentives that such a group might have to reflect the community's hostility to sex offenders and to emphasize the dangers posed by juvenile offenders as a way to justify the importance of the treatment enterprise, its need for resources, and the claims of therapists for power over their clients and over other actors in the juvenile justice system. Further, the absence of psychiatry from the professional base of the Task Force may signal that a major branch of the treatment profession is not in sympathy with the ideological preferences or factual assumptions of this Task Force.

But there is also evidence that the premises and claims of the 1993 report are widely shared in the offense-specific treatment community for juvenile sex offenders. A series of "state plans" for implementing sex-offender treatment borrows extensively from the 1988 original and 1993 revised Task Force reports. These documents do not carry official status, either, but they have been circulated for more than a decade without any sharp or sustained critique. While it is prudent to expect wide variation in the assumptions and sentiments expressed by sex therapists at the operational level, there is no reason to doubt that the 1993 report is an accurate reflection of the core beliefs of an important segment of the treatment community. If so, the phenomenon of juvenile sex-offender treatment in the Task Force invites historical and comparative inquiry. How does this Task Force's recommendations for the treatment of sex offenders compare to the ideology of juvenile justice historically or in recent times, to the treatment of mental illness and social deviance by clinical and therapeutic specialists, and to other social movements?

Comparisons and Contexts

We can first ask how the Task Force's proposals for sex-offender treatment compares with other approaches for responding to criminality and social deviance? Because the subject of the Task Force is juvenile sex offenders, the first stop on any tour of treatment ideologies should be the original "rehabilitative ideal" that was associated with the creation of juvenile courts in the United States and their administration for the first six decades of the twentieth century (Allen 1964). The original goal of treatment in the early juvenile courts was to help the delinquent or endangered child. To this end, juvenile court judges could use any of the tools available to them (including secure confinement in training schools), but always only in the child's best interests (Zimring, 1982, chap. 3).

Since the juvenile's welfare was the sole criterion for intervention, the court could be trusted to act in accord with the juvenile's best interest without the presence of any separate representative in court, like a lawyer, to speak for the child. The juvenile court judge was in effect the delinquent's advocate. Since the court usually had a better read on the child's best interest than the immature and dependent young person himself, there was no objection in the original ideology of juvenile justice to acting against the child's expressed preferences. Coercion in a good cause was not regarded as a problem.

Is this practice of acting in the child's best interests a true forebear of the foundations for juvenile sex treatment in the 1993 Task Force report? Certainly the paternalism and toleration of coercion found in original theories of juvenile justice resonate in the report (see Schlossman, 1977; Platt, 1969), but the differences in the rationale for such features are also extraordinary. For starters, the sole reason for exercising power over a juvenile in the rehabilitative logic of the original juvenile court was to help the delinquent. By contrast, the delinquent's interests are never explicitly considered in *any* of the thirteen reasons for prosecutions in juvenile court announced by the Task Force (National Adolescent Perpetrator Network, 1993, p. 19). While the controls that the Task Force seeks to impose will in its view help the youth stay out of trouble, the main reason for imposing them is community protection. No wonder arrest and prosecution were discretionary in the original rehabilitative ideal undergirding the establishment of the juvenile courts, but are mandatory in the Task Force program.

The second key difference between the two is the importance of youth as a mitigating and defining characteristic. In the omnibus theory of delinquency, the only subjects for the juvenile court are those who are too immature for blame, who can effect change in their behaviors, and who are capable of developing into solid citizens. A youth who was sophisticated and committed to criminal values was often viewed as not a fit subject for the court (Zimring, 1978). By contrast, the 1993 Task Force report makes the assumption that all its adolescent subjects are blameworthy and fully accountable for their acts. The extraordinary powers the Task Force wishes to exercise are not based on the immaturity of offenders, ensuring that the reasons for coercive controls do not end when the offenders reach maturity.

The differences between juvenile and adult offenders is of defining importance to the original juvenile court, but are hardly addressed and are of very limited evident importance in the 1993 Task Force report. That report at one point does note that juvenile offenders have fewer offenses in their histories, and expresses reservations about waiving juveniles into criminal courts. But even these reservations are not based on the harm that this might inflict on a youth, but rather "concerns which dictate caution in doing so include the lesser availability of treatment in many adult systems and the lack of a true peer group" (p. 20).

I have already mentioned that the developmental differences of young child offenders are addressed by the Task Force, but that the developmental aspects of adolescence are not. Whatever is special about being adolescent in the context of sexual offending has no prominent role in the Task Force's analysis. It is hard to think of a sharper difference between this more recent approach and the original theory of interventionist juvenile justice. Even though both theories focus on changing the life course of young offenders, they contradict each other's premises about the importance of adolescent development and about the young offender's interests as a priority.

THE CONTRAST WITH MODERN JUVENILE JUSTICE. The contrast between the worldview of the 1993 sex-offender Task Force and priorities of the modern juvenile court is even more pronounced. The modern court is cautious with its interventions, hoping that the normal processes of maturation will resolve many of the problems that produce youth crime. It worries that interventions may do more harm than good.

The 1993 Task Force, on the other hand, does not seem to believe that what it calls "sexual abuse" is a transient or transitional phenomenon. The silent assumption seems instead to be that none of the many patterns of law violation that are aggregated into the category of sexual abuse will be resolved by normal maturation. The only concessions made to adolescent treatment subjects by the Task Force concern reservations about the use of chemical agents, satiation techniques, and aversive conditioning (National Adolescent Perpetrator Network, 1993, p. 83). It is hard to imagine two more distinctive approaches to adolescent misconduct than the general perspective of the "diversionary" modern juvenile court (Zimring, 2002) and that of the 1993 Task Force.

THE CONTRAST WITH OTHER THERAPIES. There are substantial discontinuities as well between the attitudes of the 1993 Task Force toward adolescent sexual offenders and the usual orientations of mental health and social work treatment professions toward adolescent patients with conduct disorders and criminal records. The sharpest difference is the strong identification of therapists with the needs and subjective emotional well-being of their patients, even in adolescent drug and alcohol treatment programs that make confrontational demands on patients. This identification with all the interests of patients is manifest in very different attitudes toward confidentiality with regard to disclosure in therapy. Where past illegal behavior is disclosed as an encouraged part of therapy, therapists typically recognize and assert a therapist–patient privilege. The wholesale rejection of confidentiality even for past conduct is more in keeping with the attitudes of staff clinicians employed by state prisons and correctional agencies (the professional setting of four members of the participating Task Force) than of other therapists employed to serve the individuals they treat.

The attitudes and assumptions of the 1993 Task Force seem somewhat closer to confrontational stances toward adolescents marketed under the "tough love" label in recent years. But while the tone and tactics encouraged by the Task Force are certainly tough, what is again missing from the therapeutic definition is a high-priority commitment to the patient's interests. The toughness is there, but not the love.

There also does not seem to be substantial continuity between the juvenile sex therapists who date their advent to the late 1970s and the much longer tradition in psychiatry, clinical psychology, and clinical social work of treatment and counseling of juvenile sex offenders. Juvenile sex offending is by no means a recent phenomenon and has long been accompanied by clinical counseling and treatment for children and adolescents arrested as a result of sexual conduct. This history is not acknowledged by the Task Force in its 1993 report, and the contrast in tone between Lewis Doshay and his 1943 report and the 1993 manifesto is great. Doshay calls the New York clinic's adolescent clientele "boys" in the title of his book, *The Boy Sex Offender and His Later Career*. This term is both too diminutive and too positive in connotation to ever be used in the 1993 Task Force volume.

A final contrast concerns other organizations of sex-treatment professionals. There are indications that many treatment providers take a much less extreme position toward juvenile offenders than the 1993 Task Force. The board of directors of the Association for the Treatment of Sexual Abusers issued a statement on "The Effective Legal Management of Juvenile Sex Offenders" that is less punitive in orientation, more explicit in distinguishing between juvenile and adult offenders, and explicit also in preferring community treatment to the institutionalization of juvenile offenders (Association for the Treatment of Sexual Abusers, 2000). While this statement was in part provoked by the post-1994 issue of the inclusion of juveniles in sex-offender registration and notification schemes, it also appears to have been an attempt to provide an alternative to the stridency of the 1993 Task Force report.

The Roots of Adversarial Therapy

Where, then, are the roots of adversarial therapy for juvenile sex offenders in the National Task Force's manifesto? Part of the origin of adversarial sex-offender therapy is in the conflicted and cynical professional experience of the state-employed "shrink" in correctional institutional settings. Working with the disturbed and the dangerous chronic offenders in state hospitals for adults with long and apparently irreversible histories, two psychologists writing in the "nothing works" 1970s created a profile of what they called the "criminal personality (Yochelson and Samenow, 1976). The setting was Saint Elizabeth's Hospital in the District of Columbia. While this profile was never based on juvenile offenders, in its approach it was capable of migrating down the age scale to describe a blameworthy and intractable class of offender. This apparently happened in the Task Force report; Yochelson and Samenow's 1976 book is one of very few works with any criminological credentials to be found in the Task Force's list of references.

The 1993 Task Force also seems rooted in victims' rights concerns, taken to be a philosophy of criminal justice. There is, of course, no novelty in psychologists and social workers sympathizing with crime victims, but this need not influence the type of therapy or its duration chosen for the treatment of offenders. A therapist should be able to empathize with the victim and with criminal offenders in equal measure, and what is chosen or found to work therapeutically in the treatment of offenders should have no necessary connection to what makes crime victims feel vindicated.

But many in the victims' rights movement in the United States of the late 1980s and 1990s imagined the criminal justice and correctional process to be a status competition between crime victims and criminal offenders, so that citizens were asked to align themselves with one or the other group. Further, conferring benefits on offenders, in this view, was seen as a way of downgrading the importance of crime victims and their losses. At its most extreme, this approach understood victims and offenders to be engaged in a zero-sum competition in which a benefit to one side must punish the other. Thus, unlike what happens in the real world of criminal justice, any policy that harmed offenders was taken to be a good thing for crime victims. On that assumption, any incremental increase in the punishment of sex-crime offenders is assumed to have benefits (Zimring, Hawkins, & Kamin, 2001, chap. 11).

The rhetoric of the 1993 Task Force transforms the treatment community into an activist for punishment-oriented victims' rights and community safety, asserting there is no inconsistency between this activism and the commitment to the best interests of patients. The device used to create this harmony, assuming that nonrecidivism is the only interest that offenders in treatment should have, works just as well to argue that juvenile and criminal prosecution are always in any offenders' best interests, often including as well substantial incarceration. The magic word that transforms all these hardships into true benefits for offenders in the Task Force report is "accountability," and its origins in the current justice system debates is the rhetoric of victims' rights.

This reorientation toward treatment as control of juvenile sex offenders began during the same era as the sevenfold increase in imprisonment of adults for nonrape sex offenses and the fourfold increase, during the years after 1972, in overall rates of incarceration in the United States. The Task Force on juvenile sex treatment was not the only alliance between therapists and agencies made in the interests of social control in this era—drug treatment grew expansively in the 1980s and 1990s, and the conflict of interest that threatens the drug therapist who becomes a criminal justice system adjunct is not insubstantial.

I think, however, that the unmitigated hostility of the 1993 Task Force report to the juvenile sex offender sets that branch of coercive therapeutics apart even from the drug treatment approach and its clinical adherents. The tone and priorities of the 1993 report when dealing with adolescent offenders sets this theory of offense-specific treatment apart from any previous community-based therapeutic alliances with agencies of social control. While drug treatment was oriented toward providing community-based treatment for substance abuse as an alternative to punishment, the sex-treatment Task Force seems more committed to punishment *and* treatment as supplementary mechanisms of control. The 1993 Task Force approach is historically unprecedented. But in its emphatic embrace of the adversarial therapeutic approach, the National Adolescent Perpetrator Network is also very much a child of its time.

The extraordinary ideology of the Task Force is certainly not a necessary part of programs dedicated to the treatment of children and adolescents involved in sexual misconduct. Treatment and counseling programs can be designed with substantial deference to the developmental needs and legal

rights of juveniles. In chapter 6, I explore the value of treatment and counseling in juvenile justice responses to sex offenders.

But any programs of juvenile sex treatment in the early years of the
twenty-first century must take cognizance of the ideology of sex treatment
revealed by the 1993 Task Force report. Programs of treatment that are
less dismissive of the interests of adolescents and more attentive to helping them avoid stigmatization must clearly make their differences known.
In this light, the Task Force report should become a compulsory starting
point for discourse on treatment policy. The therapists and justice system
staff who deal with juvenile offenders can support or oppose the model for
treatment it sets forth, but they cannot ignore it.

Part II

Principles and Policies

_____

Chapter 5

The Sex Offender in Juvenile Court

This chapter outlines the strategic objectives and assumptions of modern juvenile courts in delinquency cases and measures these assumptions against the known facts about adolescent sex offending and offenders. The fundamental question for this analysis is whether the assumptions and objectives on the part of modern juvenile courts regarding delinquents generally are appropriate also for sex offenders who come under the court's jurisdiction. If so, then the most appropriate policy environment for such offenders is American juvenile courts, which are informed by the age-specific policies of police and probation officials and correctional agencies that have grown around such courts. But if, on the other hand, a sharp difference is found between the juvenile sex offender and the juvenile burglar, adjustments in treatment modalities and goals must be made before specific policies are designed.

Why a Juvenile Court for Crime?

Most developed nations and every jurisdiction in the United States maintain two separate judicial institutions with responsibility for adjudicating criminal charges. Criminal courts exist to adjudicate and determine sentences for criminal offenders over a stipulated age of majority, while juvenile courts (using a different nomenclature and having different sentencing options) have the same responsibility for minors. The usual statutory threshold in the United States that determines whether an accused burglar will be charged as a felon in criminal court or alleged to be a delinquent in a juvenile court proceeding is age eighteen. This "dual system" of adjudicating criminal charges has been in operation in the United States for more than a century. Prior to 1899, all criminal charges were processed in criminal courts. Today worldwide, however, very few nations continue to have such a unified system in which criminal courts are responsible for all case processing, and most of those that do exclude youth from any criminal liability until ages fourteen or fifteen (Doak, 2002, pp. 506–507).

But why two separate courts to assess liability and decide on the dispositions stemming from criminal charges, and why should an offender's age be the criterion used to sort the accused into separate judicial institutions? The justification for juvenile courts in their early years was that concepts such as "blameworthiness" and "punishment" were irrelevant in juvenile courts. The only function of such courts was to help children, whether because they were victims of parental neglect or because they posed a threat to the community by their misconduct. With this no-fault agenda, the distinction between the work of criminal courts—blame and punishment—and the orientation of juvenile courts was clear. Why children and teens in these early years of juvenile court jurisprudence were generally thought to be blameless for their misconduct was never fully articulated. Indeed, in the few cases where the juvenile court "waived" its jurisdiction over those still young enough to be tried as juveniles, criminal courts were empowered with the capacity to try and punish the young offenders (Tanenhaus, 2000). So there was no legislative judgment that all or most adolescents within the age span for juvenile court jurisdiction lacked the capacity to be held responsible for criminal acts and punished.

So the early theory about what separates the juvenile offender from the criminal defendant rested on the wholly different set of government objectives in juvenile versus criminal courts. It was the character of state policy rather than just the age difference between fifteen-year-old and nineteen-year-old burglars that justified the two separate court systems. But the only problem with this theory is that is was never true. From its earliest days, the U.S. juvenile court judges responded to young burglars with the same mixed motives that most adults have when dealing with destructive and defiant adolescent behavior. Detention and training school commitments were punitive in intent as well as in effect in 1907 just as fully as in recent years. A jurisprudence of the juvenile court that insisted that how they disposed of cases was solely a function of the best interests of youthful burglars and purse snatchers were transparently disingenuous. Perhaps some judges and probation officers believed such rhetoric, but no delinquents did (Schlossman, 1977; Zimring, 1978).

By 1967, when the U.S. Supreme Court held in *In re Gault*, 387 U.S. 1 (1967), that juvenile court proceedings that put delinquents at risk of secure confinement must provide them with lawyers, notice of charges, and other procedural protections, it was clear that the decisions by American juvenile courts often involved elements of punishment and blame. But if the court for children was in the punishment business, what after all was different enough about juvenile and criminal courts to justify two separate court systems responding to criminal behavior? When *In Re Gault* was decided, the dominant philosophy in criminal courts was a mix of punishment and rehabilitation. After *Gault* stripped away the pretense that juvenile courts served only the needs of those brought before it, what could justify a separate court for the society's youngest criminal offenders?

Plenty, it seems. In the generation since the Supreme Court handed down its seminal decision protecting the rights of due process for adolescent offenders, the juvenile court has continued to function separately in all fifty states and the District of Columbia. While legislation in many states cut back slightly on juvenile court jurisdiction in some serious criminal cases (Zimring, 1998), only New York (1978) and Florida (1979) have cut back significantly on the delinquency jurisdiction of juvenile courts in the post-*Gault* era. Why is that?

The most plausible justification for a special court for the youngest offenders is a consensus on the part of the public that young offenders are different, and that responding to youth crime calls for two policies that differ from typical criminal court responses. In the first place, the immaturity that is characteristic of youth is associated with lower levels of culpability for the same criminal acts, and with different configurations of culpability for peer group-centered criminal behavior that is typical of the early and middle teens. Diminished responsibility is not by itself a reason for a separate court system for youth, of course, but expertise in dealing with youth crime may favor a specialist court.

The second reason for a special policy toward young offenders relates not to the personal culpability of young offenders but to the societal investment in giving young people, even young offenders, a chance to grow into normal adulthoods. This "room to reform" rationale favors punishments for youth crime that do not permanently damage the young offender's future life opportunities (Zimring, 1978, 1982). It is widely believed that the large number of adolescents who violate the law and the high rates of teen offending are transitory phenomena associated with a transitional status and life period (Elliot, 1994). This transitional theory of adolescent offending provides a clear rationale for a "room to reform" policy: even absent heroic interventions, the criminality associated with adolescence will level off as adolescents achieve adult roles and status.

There are three implications of this approach to youth crime as a developmental phenomenon. First, it regards criminal offenses as a more-or-less expected aspect of adolescent development, a by-product of the same transitional pressures that increase rates of traffic accidents, sexual risk-taking, and depression. Youth crime is not a welcome part of adolescent development but it is regarded as a natural risk of a stressful period.

The second implication of the notion that high rates of adolescent crime are a developmental phenomenon that can be weathered with time is that major interventions may not be necessary to halt the progression of criminal behavior from adolescence to chronic adult recidivism. The central assertion of what has been called "adolescence limited" offending (Moffitt, 1993) is that the cure for much youth crime is the offender's growing up.

Related to the hope of desistance from crime as a normal part of development into adulthood is a reluctance to use expensive or potentially destructive crime countermeasures that may not be needed to avoid chronic offending in the long run. Punishment for wrongdoing is appropriate as long as the developmental opportunities of the young offender are not hindered. But interventions that threaten long-term damage are disfavored. Short-term detentions are quite common in American juvenile courts, indeed much too common, but long-term commitments to secure confinement are a rarely used last resort that can only be justified when all other means of controlling dangerous behavior have failed.

The developmental hazard of long-term confinement is that it hinders the ability of those confined to grow up and grow out of criminogenic adolescent behavior. There may be circumstances in which drastic punishments are required, but such punishments are always imposed at the cost of violating important elements of youth-development policy. By design, then, the juvenile justice system is biased against sanctions that interrupt and disrupt adolescent development. This is one reason why long-term confinement is much more common in criminal than in juvenile courts (Zimring, 2002, fig. 5.1).

There have been some changes over time in the emphasis on diversion and caution in delinquency policy. The middle third of the twentieth century was a period of optimism about the potential of programmed interventions to accomplish more good than harm. With decline in confidence about the effectiveness of behavior therapies, the emphasis over the last thirty years has shifted from therapeutic programs to natural developmental processes, from the juvenile court as a place that coordinates forceful interventions in the lives of delinquents to a more cautious court that seeks to divert delinquents from the harmfully punitive processes of criminal courts while they mature out of their criminal propensities. Even as explicitly punitive responses are seen more often in juvenile courts, there is much less confidence in modern juvenile courts that locking teenaged defendants up is a good way of helping them.

Sex in the Juvenile Court

The preceding section described the general orientation of juvenile courts toward delinquents. But to what extent has the court's general orientation informed its policies and decisions about sexual misconduct? Without attempting a history of sex offenders in American juvenile justice, four points can be made about the treatment of sexual offenses in the first century of the American juvenile court. The first is that the attitude of the juvenile justice system toward delinquency as a general phenomenon was almost always the major influence on how the juvenile court treated sex cases in its first century of existence. During periods of heavy emphasis on intervention, juvenile court judges were apt to institutionalize sexually active girls, either as delinquent or "beyond control." As confidence in the propriety and effectiveness of coercive treatment for status offenders diminished, the "deinstitutionalization of status offenders"—efforts to keep disobedient teens out of locked institutions—became a major focus of reform in the 1970s. The heyday of programmatic juvenile justice was a period also for Lewis Doshay and his sex-offender clinic in New York. As belief in programmatic treatments grew less enthusiastic, the creation of new sex-offender programs within the juvenile court was also in decline. For most of its history, the programmatic tilt in juvenile court policy toward sex offenders usually reflected the general fashions in juvenile justice.

But a second salient fact about policy toward sex offenders in juvenile courts is that it has not been a very important emphasis throughout the court's history. Particularly for males, sex was never anywhere near as important for juvenile courts as it was for juveniles. As chapter 3 reported, sex cases average 2 percent of the current caseloads in modern juvenile courts. A recent law school casebook on juvenile justice has no entry for sex offenses or sex offenders in its index, while there are nineteen entries for status offenders (Feld, 2000, pp. 901–905). The sex offender and sex offense are also missing from the nineteen-page index of a comprehensive reference work on juvenile justice (Rosenheim et al., 2002, pp. 535–554). Yet the criminal law and the definition of delinquency both have broad prescriptions of adolescent sexual behavior that could have justified extensive involvement in the sexual lives of American adolescents. In this respect, a major incursion into the sex lives of American adolescents is one natural offshoot of an interventionist approach to juvenile justice that has not happened for males.

There was, however, one exception to this low priority the juvenile courts accorded to sex—namely, the campaign to rescue female status offenders, which is the third noteworthy point in the history of sex in juvenile court. The omnibus theory of delinquency did not require that minors commit crimes before delinquency jurisdiction could be assumed. Being "beyond control" or "in danger of living an immoral life" could be a sufficient condition for use of major sanctions. This potential power was used against girls who were regarded as sexually at risk in the most famous of the juvenile court's twentieth-century moral crusades:

> For cultural and biological reasons relating to the risk of pregnancy, parents and police are more prone to disapprove of female than of male sexuality, and judges are more prone to be "protective" of young women than young men. . . . As a result, young women—who rarely faced delinquency charges—made up a substantial portion of the juvenile court's status offense docket. . . . Indeed, they were likelier to spend more time in institutions than were young men who had committed criminal acts. (Teitelbaum, 2002, pp. 163–164)

The result of this effort to use coercive controls to reduce sexual risk was, by common consensus, the most prominent failure of the first seven decades of American juvenile courts. Blue-ribbon commissions and the federal legislature worked hard in seeking to reduce the powers of juvenile court to commit status offenders to institutions, and the Institute of Judicial Administration "recommended the elimination of general juvenile court jurisdiction over status offenders" (Teitelbaum, 2002, p. 166).

Part of the problem with juvenile justice's first crusade for sexual morals was the use of force against young persons who were not harming others, a principled objection that does not apply to offenders who commit assaults or who have sexual contact with much younger children. But another reason for distrusting coercive interventions was the failure of coerced cures to make a critical difference in the conduct of their targets, and this lack of program payoff may be relevant to sex-offender treatment.

One reason the interventions for status offenders were not cost effective is that they often were not needed; in Teitelbaum's words, "We know that most adolescents who misbehave when they are young do not become adult deviants and ultimately get exactly what they deserve—their own children." But six decades of experience had also convinced observers that "we have found little that effectively persuades adolescents to conform to commands or even to good advice" (Teitelbaum, 2002, p. 173). And this experience would seem quite relevant to current concerns about programs for adolescent sexual offenders.

The fourth point worth noting about the recent history of sex-offender policy in the juvenile court is that the juvenile courts themselves appear to think that the policies and sanctions of the juvenile court are suitable for sex offenders. Figure 5.1 shows the percentage of all felony charges in Texas during 1988 in which prosecutors requested and judges granted motions to transfer juveniles to criminal courts. Because any felony charge can provide the basis for a waiver request, a motion could be made (and granted) in all the cases reported in the figure. The data come from a study of judicial waiver in Texas by Robert Dawson (1992).

The sex category reported in the 1992 study, "Sex Assault," includes all behavior covered in forcible rape arrests and charges and a variety of less serious charges. Dawson finds that prosecutors requested a transfer to the arena of larger penalties and adult-style procedures of criminal courts in only 2.9 percent of all sex-assault cases. When compared to other serious changes, prosecutors thought that juvenile court was inappropriate in ten times as many homicide charges and twice as often when robbery was charged as in sex assaults. Texas juvenile court judges regarded that court as the appropriate venue for 98 percent of sex-assault charges.

What separates the 2 percent of sexual-assault charges that are transferred to the criminal court is probably some combination of the seriousness of the current charge and the criminal record of the accused that convince the prosecutor and the court that substantial punishment will be required. The low rate of transfer requests suggests that there is nothing about the sex-offense category that is believed to be inconsistent with the normal processes and assumptions of juvenile justice. But one cannot derive any more specific conclusions about the jurisprudence of sex offenses in juvenile court from the absence of larger rates of punitive response. Are there more specific indications in the literature of delinquency and juvenile justice of approaches to adolescent offenses and offenders?

The Jurisprudence of Juvenile Sex Crimes

While the literature on the topic of sex crimes in juvenile justice is modest at best, there are clear indications in that literature that (a) patterns of sexual offending among children and youth have been consistent through-

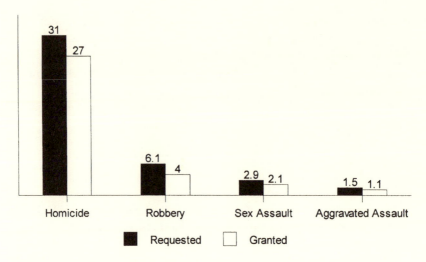

Figure 5.1. Rates of transfer requests and transfer motions granted in felony charges against juveniles in Texas during 1988
Source: Dawson 1992, table 4, p. 988, table 8, p. 1013.

out the history of the juvenile court, and (b) most juvenile sex offenders historically have been considered normal and nonthreatening parts of the juvenile court caseload.

One early and worldly analysis of the category is found in the classic 1916 book by Bernard Flexner and Roger Baldwin, *Juvenile Courts and Probation.* Concerning "special cases," the authors wrote:

> Another group of cases diversely treated are those involving some sexual wrong-doing—the rather frequent instances of maturing boys attempting intercourse with very little girls, or vulgar practices between boys and girls in the very early period of adolescence. There is no reason why such cases should be regarded as subjects for peculiar and severe treatment. These sex offenses do not indicate abnormalities. There is hardly any boy in the uncertain revolutionary years of adolescence who would not become involved under certain conditions and temptations. It is the common opinion of workers with children that very few such cases are ever discovered compared with the number which actually exist and very few of those discovered are brought to the juvenile court. Says a prominent judge, "If the case is not one of chronic sex viciousness, it is perfectly absurd to commit the child to an institution, and it should never be done. Many of these

cases are physical rather than moral, or, in a sense, unmoral. It is only in a case of sex viciousness that is apparently chronic and dangerous to society and other children where commitment should be had. Feeling, of course, is often high in neighborhoods where such acts have been discovered, but the court can meet such situations without recourse to institutions. The boy's family itself is usually only too glad to move" (Flexner and Balwin, 1916, pp. 77–78).

The profile of offenders and victims that Flexner and Baldwin described, "maturing boys attempting intercourse with very little girls or vulgar practices . . . in the very early period of adolescence" are precisely parallel to the reported arrest patterns for current cases examined in chapter 3. And the reasons for avoiding "peculiar and severe treatment" in such cases are in no sense because the behavior is regarded as either innocent or harmless. Instead, the view of probation experts in 1916 was that no special pathological condition was implicated in these cases, and the important distinction for sanctioning purposes was between acts of wrongdoing that "do not indicate abnormalities" and cases of "sex viciousness that is apparently chronic and dangerous to society and other children."

What made juvenile institutions and extensive clinical interactions unnecessary in the view of Flexner and Balwin was not a shoulder-shrugging belief that "boys were being boys" in the sense that their offending conduct was harmless, but the absence of any commitment to deviant values on the part of the offender. The wrongfulness of the conduct was not only recognized by Flexner and Baldwin but also by the offenders. Without any commitment to deviant values, the sex offenders were not a moral challenge to conventional values. Since they also did not exhibit any deviant sexual urges, these offenders were not in danger of chronic sexual offense in the future. This emphasis on values was quite consistent with the sociological orientation toward delinquency and toward delinquents of the early years of the juvenile court.

A generation after Flexner and Baldwin, Lewis Doshay brought extensive statistical data to his analysis of the "boy sex offender" but reached conclusions that were, if anything, more cheerful than those of Flexner and Baldwin: "Male juvenile sex delinquency is self-curing, providing the latent forces of shame and guilt . . . are properly stimulated into action" (Doshay, 1943, p. 168). Doshay was an enthusiastic proponent of brief treatment programs that included active family cooperation. Referral to the court clinic studied involved an average of two or three visits over a very short period of time. Just under half of the young offenders visited the clinic only once and were not supervised thereafter (p. 86). "Sharp criticism of the juvenile by parents or guardians is uncalled for, *and spying on the boy should be avoided*" (p. 174, italics in the original).

While Doshay was a psychiatrist, the theory of sex-offender etiology and control that he advanced had important sociological dimensions. What made the sex offender with no other signs of delinquent orientation so easy to rehabilitate was the boy's own understanding of the wrongfulness of his sexual conduct. The primary mechanism to avoid future sex misconduct was the offender's own moral sense.

The major distinction among types of boy sex offenders in Doshay's analysis was between subjects who only had committed a sex offense and what Doshay called the "mixed" offenders, those with other types of delinquent behavior on their records. These mixed-offense boys were much more likely to commit further offenses, though mostly not of a sexual nature. The important distinction between the "sex only" and "mixed" groups was the stronger evidence of delinquent values (and probably delinquent peers) in the mixed group. This generated a much higher likelihood of future unlawful behavior, but only minimal risk of future sexual illegality. The Doshay schema was theoretically clear and empirically well established by the New York data. It concluded there was but a low level of paraphilia in the population of juvenile sex offenders.

The findings about juvenile sex offenders by observers like Flexner, Baldwin, and Doshay fit nicely with the general theories of juvenile justice popular at midcentury as well as later in the history of the juvenile court. Even if the condition required some treatment, sexual offending was not a challenge to the general approach of the juvenile court or to its institutions so long as the threatening conditions were regarded as neither extraordinarily serious nor a prelude to chronic adult offending.

The Current Scene

The remarkable thing about contemporary writing on juvenile sex offenders by academic specialists in juvenile justice or juvenile court judges is that there isn't any. The longest publication by far on the topic in a juvenile justice journal is the 1993 report of the National Task Force discussed in chapter 4. Although that report appeared in a journal geared to juvenile court judges, no juvenile court judges had any hand in its preparation. What one encounters is not so much a paucity of scholarly literature on juvenile sex offenders by juvenile justice experts as a void.

Part of the explanation for this void comes from the marginal status of sex offenses in the business of the court. Much of the gap is a function of the decline over the last generation in scholarly studies of juvenile justice of all kinds. But there has been no dialogue among legal scholars or judges about the special characteristics and special problems of sex offenders in juvenile court and there has been little specific documentation of patterns of decisionmaking in sex cases. No longitudinal studies of sex cases in juvenile court have been published, and there is no systematic comparison of sex cases with other cases at various decision points in the juvenile justice process. Some aggregate statistics are available on dispositions in sex cases, but trends over time are not determinable. For example, the Federal Office of Juvenile Justice and Delinquency Prevention has published one-day counts of juveniles in residential placement for sex offenses. This total was 4,665 in 1997 and 5,643 in 2001 (see figure 4.3). Whether this increase over four years is a trend or a cyclical fluctuation is not known. Much more research could and should be done concerning the determinants of outcomes in the juvenile court's sex-offender cases.

The Calculus of Dispositional Decisionmaking

As far as we know, the methodology of responding to juvenile sex offending was and is the same balancing act the court must perform as in other cases of serious criminal offenses by youth within its jurisdiction. The developmental needs and prospects of the delinquent must be measured against the seriousness of the offense and the minimum punitive response that is required to accommodate the concerns of the court and the community. While punishments may be imposed, special efforts are made to avoid compromising the offender's opportunity to mature without permanent disadvantage.

A second constraint on limited responses to juvenile sex offending is concern about the potential dangerousness of the offender. Putting aside short-term detention, secure confinement is a juvenile court sanction that usually reflects a concern that the offender's release to the community would pose a high risk of serious re-offending. The calculus of weighing dangerousness against the harmful aspects of secure confinement is similar for the juvenile who robs, who steals cars, and who sexually offends. The distinctive feature of the sex offender is that the concern is generally about future sex offenses rather than a wider range of offenses.

The major decision that the juvenile court makes in serious sex cases is the same as that made in any other serious offense—the choice between secure confinement and community-based supervision and dispositional conditions. Putting pretrial detention aside again, the presumption in the majority of cases in juvenile court is that offenders are best placed in community settings. For sex offenders, some type of treatment or counseling program is likely to be imposed either in an institution (if that is where the delinquent is placed) or in the community (the more common outcome). The types of programs vary widely, particularly with respect to the number and sort of auxiliary controls they involve. Juvenile sex-offender treatment ranges from low-intensity group counseling sessions to aggressive use of polygraphic testing to police and prosecute further offenses. Consequently, the distinctions between forms of offender counseling and treatment are more important than whether some form of treatment is part of a juvenile's disposition plan. The huge variation in treatment components is an open invitation to compare the outcomes associated with different treatment conditions. But no rigorous comparative assessments have yet been reported.

The Changing Environment

While the general principles governing disposition in sex cases may not have changed much, there have been a series of shifts in the environment in which American juvenile courts operate that have influenced juvenile court decisions in sex cases since the mid-1980s, and likely will continue to do so.

The first major change in the decisional environment of American juvenile justice is the increased role and power of prosecutors. One natural result of the larger role that *In re Gault* created for defense lawyers in juvenile courts was that public prosecutors also began to play a more prominent part in charging, trying, and making dispositional decisions in juvenile courts (Feld, 1999). The prosecutor's growing power has come at the expense of the authority previously endowed in judicial and probationary officials. With the increasing role of the prosecutor there has been a shift from emphasis on treatment needs to using criteria of crime seriousness to identify priority cases. The larger the role of prosecutors, the more similar are the priorities and outcomes in juvenile and criminal courts.

But while the power of prosecutors in the juvenile justice system has expanded dramatically over the past two decades, there is still an extraordinary contrast between the authority of judicial and probationary officials in juvenile versus criminal courts. The hegemony of prosecutors in criminal courts is much greater than in any major juvenile justice system in the

United States, while the relative powers of judges and probation staff are very much greater in juvenile courts.

For sex offenses and sex offenders, the most likely impact of increased prosecutorial power is an increased emphasis on cases that are regarded as most serious. This has been reflected in the higher volume of cases in which older juveniles are transferred to criminal courts (Fagan & Zimring, 2000), and in increased prosecutorial pressure for custodial sentences in juvenile court, either to training schools or residential treatment programs.

A second change in the environment of sex cases in juvenile courts has been the growth of juvenile sex-offender treatment programs, both residential and community based, that numbered in the hundreds in the United States by the early 1990s. The materials discussed in chapter 4 show that one major branch of the treatment groups have emphasized both the severity of juvenile sex offending and the danger posed by sex offenders (at least by those not treated) as reasons for supporting treatment modalities that monitor behavior by polygraphic testing and family reporting. While the new prosecutorial presence is felt most strongly in its emphasis on offense severity, the push from treatment personnel and clinically oriented probation reports is to emphasize concerns about future danger. Although the empirical studies undermine confidence in predicting danger, the clinical prediction of dangerousness is probably an important element in the sex-offender dispositional decisions that are made each day in the American juvenile justice system.

A third environmental shift beginning in the 1980s and 1990s has been the increase in public alarm over the sexual victimization of children. Reliable data on the incidence and prevalence of childhood sex-crime victimization does not exist, but there is no reason to suppose that the rate of such injuries fluctuates in the cyclical fashion that characterizes public concern about the molestation of children. Some of the major public landmarks of recent concern about child victimization include the McMartin preschool child molestation trial in the 1980s (Eberle, 1993), a number of extraordinary and publicized civil and criminal prosecutions based on the recovered memories in adulthood of child victims and witnesses many years later, and the homicide victimizations that produced the push for Megan's Laws, which I discuss in chapter 7. There had been periods before when citizens were prompted to worry about the sexual victimization of children. In the 1940s and 1950s, for example, even in the face of low and stable rates of violent crime, J. Edgar Hoover wrote articles warning parents that "the nation's women and children will never be secure . . . so long as degenerates run wild" (Hoover, 1947, 1955).

The stereotypical sexual predators during periods of public panic are almost never juveniles, but the attention to childhood victimization spills over into policies that have a direct impact on younger offenders, such as Megan's Laws, and may also result in a tendency to regard most forms of childhood sexual victimization, including offenses by juveniles, as more dangerous and serious than they actually are.

The tone of the sex treatment orientation discussed in chapter 4 is a potential challenge to the images of moderate culpability and transitory risk that produce a comfortable fit with modern theories of juvenile justice. If juvenile sex offenders are so much a threat to community safety that the interests of the offender in a normal development to adulthood should be disregarded, this will put enormous pressure on the personnel of juvenile courts. If the policies that juvenile courts are asked to carry out include lifetime stigma or extended incapacitation, such policies will clash with the canons of juvenile development that are of central importance to theories of juvenile justice. So whether juvenile courts are appropriate places for processing most adolescent sex offenders depends in large part on appropriate policies toward juvenile sexual offenses and sexual offenders under 18.

The following two chapters cover the two most important policy domains that constitute modern legal policies toward adolescent offenders. Chapter 6 addresses dispositions for adolescent sex offenders in juvenile and criminal courts, with particular attention to the content of counseling and treatment programs. Chapter 7 discusses the shape and impact of legal requirements of registration and community notification as they apply to adolescent sex offenders. These collateral policies may have more significant consequences than any of the direct sanctions imposed by the court.

Chapter 6

Reform in Juvenile Court

The main goal of this chapter is to use the known facts about juvenile sex offending as the basis for proposing reforms in juvenile court policies toward sexual offenses and offenders. But the chapter begins with a more typical academic ploy—a research agenda for filling gaps in the knowledge base about children and adolescents who commit sex offenses. The first section of the chapter addresses three key issues that research must resolve in the near future. The second section considers the basic principles and policies that are appropriate to responding to the three different classes of sex offenders in the juvenile justice system identified in chapter 3. I then explore a series of more detailed legal and policy questions that concern the juvenile sex offender.

A Policy Research Agenda

The most predictable cliché in any academic treatment of a topic is the plea for more research. Too often, a plan for data collection is put forward as an alternative to making difficult policy choices, often as an alternative to any more immediate action. That is certainly not my intention in this chapter. But answering three concrete research questions *must* become part of a rational legal policy process if we are to effectively and appropriately respond to child and adolescent sex offenders:

- What are the middle- and long-term risks of sexual re-offending associated with the major varieties of juvenile sex offending?
- What characteristics of offenders and offenses are associated with significantly higher levels of sexual re-offending, and to what extent is future

sexual offending predictable even in the highest adolescent risk categories frequently encountered?
- What is the effect of low- and moderate-intensity sex-offender treatment programs on the likelihood that typical juvenile sex offenders will sexually re-offend?

Measuring the Risks of Juvenile Recidivism

The first basic policy need in measuring the risks associated with juvenile sex offending is construction of base expectancy rates for children and adolescents apprehended for various types of offenses. In chapter 3 we saw that very few studies of juvenile offenders carefully follow representative populations of adolescents apprehended for sex offenses. Only a few case disposition studies reported in that chapter provided middle-term follow-up on offender samples as a whole rather than only a subset of the offender population that was referred to clinical treatment programs. Most published research reports on small and unrepresentative subsets of the juvenile offender population.

The majority of good sample follow-ups such as Weinrot's three-court sample and the Texas Youth Authority release cohort were not published in journals, and the follow-up periods for these samples were usually not sufficient. Yet the first important question for juvenile sex-offender policy concerns the average or aggregate sex-offense recidivism rate. There is now a sharp contrast between the rhetoric of some juvenile treatment clinicians and the best statistics compiled on juvenile offenders. While I am comfortable preferring the current data to the rhetoric of juvenile dangerousness, a better path is to spend a few years and a modest budget obtaining a long-range, multisite measure of recidivism for sex offenses and other offenses among broad samples of juvenile offenders. While some self-reports from subsamples of juvenile offenders would help determine which sorts of behavior generate apprehensions, even carefully collected data documenting only re-arrest and reconviction rates for large and representative samples of juvenile sex offenders would represent a major step forward.

An empirical foundation of this sort can provide policymakers with an actuarial basis for creating developmentally specific policies directed toward adolescent sexual offenders. The two largest categories of acts that lead to arrest of young adolescents—sexual abuse of younger children by younger teens and sexual assault of peers—are conduct categories where we know that the etiology and clinical significance of the behavior is quite different for adolescent and adult. But often perceptions of the danger of juvenile sex offending are based on demonstrably false analogies with adult models and adult probabilities. Without a separate knowledge base that is specific to adolescence, both the legislator and the clinician will frequently rely on such false premises.

Seeking the Determinants of Future Danger in Juvenile Sex Offending

Whatever the differences between adolescent and adult patterns of sexual offending, there can be little doubt that some young sex offenders are likely to commit future sexual offenses, and some adolescent offenders pose a threat for the commission of the most serious forms of juvenile sex crime. The rate of sex-related killings among teens is very low, but it is not zero. The direct linkage between visible adolescent conduct and adult proclivities cannot be assumed from current research findings, but neither can it be dismissed. We do know that most juvenile sex offenders neither re-offend sexually while in the juvenile system nor become chronic sex offenders as adults. Because the majority of juvenile offenders are not dangerous, any attempt to discover young offenders who do present high danger must seek to identify subtypes of persons or offenses that can be distinguished in advance.

An analogy can be made here with the efforts in criminology and psychology to distinguish what the psychologist Terrie Moffitt calls "adolescent limited" juvenile delinquents from a second category of person with higher rates of recidivism for longer periods of time—what she calls "life course persistent" offenders (Moffitt, 1993). The efforts to distinguish the behavioral antecedents to long-term chronic offenders from those related to adolescent-limited careers have emphasized for the most part high rates of juvenile offending producing long official records, early age of onset of relatively serious behavior, and pathological social and home environments. But even with these multiple indicators, the efforts to isolate a category of truly high-rate criminal offenders have not produced much predictive efficiency (Greenwood and Turner, 1987; Blumstein et al., 1986).

The prediction of high rate and chronic sexual offending from juvenile behavior will probably be more difficult than using nonsexual youth criminality to predict adult offending for two reasons. First, the base rate of general criminality is much higher than the officially recorded sex offending that must be predicted in adulthood. Searching for predictors of events that have very low base rates is usually more difficult than predicting more common outcomes.

The second problem is that there is less continuity of motive, less similarity of situational pressure and opportunity, between many forms of adolescent and adult sex offending than there is between adolescent and adult street robbery or burglary. When fifteen-year-olds impose themselves sexually on younger children, they usually are not reflecting a sexual orientation that strongly prefers prepubescent targets, so a broader set of sexual opportunities as the adolescent matures will reduce the pressure to express sexual needs on forbidden targets or in ways otherwise prohibited by the criminal law. If a much larger proportion of those adults with child victims are pedophiles, it is much harder not to link the offender's sexual urges and behaviors prohibited by the criminal law.

The types of prediction exercise necessary to assess juvenile offenders at risk must start with representative samples of those juvenile sex offenders processed by juvenile courts, because it is only the prediction of the future danger of those offenders who are seen in the system that is of importance in framing policy. Patterns noted in smaller groups of juvenile clinical or institutional subjects are useful for generating hypotheses to be tested. But the laboratory for the prediction of future dangerousness of juvenile sex offenders is the juvenile justice system, and only the facts that can be determined by juvenile courts and treatment staff can be the basis for useful predictions.

The only clear predictors that have been identified to date are the number of victimizations that can be tied to a particular young offender. The selection of young male targets has been linked to deviant sexual arousal but not consistently to juvenile sex recidivism (Caldwell, 2002). Many of the adult indicators of instability and risk in sex offenders such as "subject not married" have no predictive significance in age groups where not being married is normal but sex recidivism is low.

Without adolescent-specific empirical findings on future danger, clinical predictions about juvenile offenders will continue to be scientifically bankrupt. Some have expressed confidence in the capacity of future juvenile research to produce robust findings (e.g., Caldwell, 2002), but there are no persuasive behavioral models that establish identifiable subgroups of offenders with highly predictable adult sex-offender careers. With low base rates, the sample sizes necessary to generate substantial numbers of the all-important subgroups of juvenile sex offenders must be quite large. This will not be inexpensive research. Yet a definitive test of the capacity to predict recidivism among subgroups of juveniles would be worth its considerable costs.

Pending any definitive study of future dangerousness, one by-product of a conditional information sharing scheme of the type I outline in chapter 7 would be to provide good data on the overlap between official records of juvenile sex offending and official adult sex offending. It is currently believed that about half of all adult sex offenders self-report the onset of criminal sexual behavior during adolescence. It was pointed out in chapter 3 that this finding cannot be taken as evidence that a large number of future adult offenders are classified as sex offenders in juvenile courts because the fraction of adolescent onset offenders officially identified was not known. But an information sharing system that releases juvenile records of those adults later convicted of serious sex offenses will be able to provide at nominal cost a retrospective account of the proportion of the rapists and child molesters later registered in the adult system who had official juvenile records as well. This is by no means as important as the forward-looking prediction of future danger, but it would be more accurate than the current numbers in circulation. Setting the record straight on this question is not a high priority for research but, again, such a modest undertaking is worth its low cost.

Putting Juvenile Sex-Offender Treatment to the Test

No scientifically reliable evidence is available on whether *any* type of juvenile sex-offender treatment reduces the likelihood of sexual re-offending. The argument is made that the low recidivism rates exhibited by juveniles who successfully complete treatment programs is evidence of treatment effectiveness (see Alexander, 1999), but the problem with any inference of treatment effects from such data is that the expected recidivism of this group in the absence of treatment is not known. Those studies that have compared treatment successes with juveniles who were not treated are also not strong evidence of program effectiveness because of the notorious difficulties of matching to treated groups. This is exacerbated when only treatment successes are compared to untreated "matches." The fact that one journal-published study (Boirduin et al., 1990) reports that it used random assignment to test and control groups but claims a 75 percent recidivism rate for untreated juvenile controls—about ten times the usual juvenile re-arrest rate—does not inspire confidence in the genre!

The obvious solution to the paucity of reliable data on the nature and magnitude of treatment effectiveness is controlled experimentation. The 1993 report of the National Adolescent Perpetrator Network (see chapter 4), however, argues that the classical method of randomly assigning subjects to treatment and nontreatment groups might unfairly deprive offenders assigned to the untreated group of the opportunity to be rescued from future sexual offending if treatment is effective. This is not a trivial objection, even if the efficacy of such treatment programs is currently unknown. Are the only alternatives weak matched-group arguments for treatment effects or rigorous studies that deprive many of their subjects of potentially important benefits?

For sex-offender treatment programs that take place in community settings, the dilemma is a false one and a rigorous test of the efficacy of coerced community-based treatment is waiting to be implemented. For treatment programs inside locked juvenile institutions, the prospects are less promising.

The design for a controlled experiment in community-based sex-offender treatment requires a big city juvenile justice system with a large number of juvenile sex arrests and with a cooperating juvenile court. Youthful sex offenders who require secure confinement because of the seriousness of their offenses would be excluded from eligibility. All juvenile sex offenders eligible for community treatment would be randomly assigned to one of two program conditions. Group A members would all be assigned to standard sex treatment as a condition of probation. The only way around the requirement of treatment would be to refuse it, which violates probation terms and risks secure confinement. All members of Group A, even if they drop out of program participation or refuse it, would be considered as part of the treatment group for follow-up purposes.

Group B members would also be placed on probation, but on the condition that they participate in community service or some other punitive intermediate-sanction program favored by the local juvenile court (see Morris & Tonry, 1990). Work crews, restitution programs, job training, and community service are some of the many intermediate-sanction programs frequently used for juveniles. Refusal to participate in the nontreatment program by this group would violate terms of probation. The Group B juveniles would also be offered sex-offender treatment, but participating in the treatment program would not relieve them of the community service duties to which they were assigned. There would be no rewards for entering treatment and no penalties for not doing so.

The test for treatment effectiveness would be the recidivism to sex offenses among all those assigned to Group A compared with the aggregate recidivism to sex offenses for all those in Group B. The comparison would test the coercion to treatment and the much higher rate of participation in sex-offender treatment in Group A. While the test versus control comparison would understate the gross magnitude of treatment effects to the extent that treated Group B volunteers had lower recidivism caused by treatment, it would provide a powerful test of the preventive potential of treatment programs.

This would not be a "do or die" test for all types of sex-offender treatment programs. There is a role for some forms of juvenile sex-offender counseling whether or not such programs demonstrably reduce the recidivism to sex offenses of those young offenders counseled. If an all-treatment group has the same re-arrest rates as youth assigned to other intermediate-sanction programs, there are still good reasons to involve first-time sex offenders in counseling programs that do not stigmatize, humiliate, or otherwise injure subjects. It is only the aversive and injurious forms of intervention that would require evidence of differential effectiveness to offset their obvious costs.

So it is likely that the rigorous testing of juvenile sex-offender treatment, now at least a decade overdue, would have a more substantial influence on the style and content of juvenile offender programs than on the rate at which some programming is used for youthful offenders. There are forms of counseling suitable for juvenile sex offenders who are at a low risk for re-offending that might benefit all subjects, regardless of the effects on recidivism; but more aversive types of intervention are not warranted unless the danger of sex recidivism is high and the efficacy of intervention is well established. A major problem with the wide variety of programs that are now described as treatments for juvenile sex offending is a blurring of the important distinctions between different types of treatment, which can result in the use of more intrusive interventions than is justified. It is literally the case that there are greater differences among types of juvenile sex-offender treatment than there are differences between extreme forms of treatment and unmitigated penal confinement. A controlled experiment is a first step toward creating a rational continuum of programs of juvenile-offender treatment.

A Framework for Juvenile Sex-Offender Policy

This chapter aims to clear the way for a reformed jurisprudence of the juvenile court response to children and adolescents who commit sexual offenses. In this section, I put forward a set of four general principles as a broad framework for the legal system's response to juvenile sex offenders. The final section explores a series of specific issues of detail that arise in the sanctioning and assessment of youths who commit sex offenses.

General Guidelines

The first installment for a framework for juvenile sex-offender policy concerns the division of responsibility among prosecutors, the juvenile court, and treatment staff in making decisions about the prosecution and disposition of juvenile sex offenders. The power to decide whether and how juveniles charged with sexual offenses should be prosecuted, petitioned, and adjudicated should be shared by judges and prosecutors in the same manner as it is in cases featuring robberies, burglaries, and assaults. This issue arises in response to the Juvenile Sex Offender Task Force report discussed in chapter 4, which advocates shifting the responsibility for dispositional determinations from prosecutors and judges to treatment staff by *requiring* prosecution in juvenile sex cases.

Even in the era before sex-offender registration laws raised the stakes of sex-offense adjudication, the Task Force recommendation for compulsory reporting and prosecution of sexual offenders represented a major shift in the juvenile justice process, without an adequate rationale. Why should prosecutorial and judicial discretions that exist for serious nonsexual crimes be suspended for juvenile sex offenses? And what is the function of a clinical assessment of a juvenile sex offender who presents no evidence of a particular sexual disorder? So a good case was never made for the mass processing of all sex complaints through the juvenile justice system. The long shadow of Megan's Laws discussed in the next chapter simply makes what was always a bad idea into a worse one in those jurisdictions where juvenile records have unconditional consequences.

If dispositions in juvenile sex cases are to remain legal rather than clinical decisions, what are the standards that should govern the choice of sanctions? The first point that requires underscoring is that juvenile sex cases are poor candidates for "fixed-price," "presumptive," or offense-based dispositional decisions. The heterogeneity of juvenile sex offenses in terms of the harm done, the offender's capacities, the extent of exploitation, the role of situational pressures, and the presence or absence of force or significant threat of violence makes it one of the least-appropriate categories of juvenile offenses and offenders for fixed-price sentencing. Dispositional decisions should be made one at a time by the same mix of intake, prosecution, and judicial staff as are responsible for dispositions in other delinquency cases. But this is not a plea for unprincipled discretion. The fact that decisions must be made on an individualized basis neither requires nor excuses the absence of principles to help identify appropriate sanctions for sex offenders.

The general calculus for the prosecution and sentencing of juvenile sex offenders is the same as that used in any other delinquency case of any seriousness: balancing a commitment to normal youth development against considerations of desert and personal dangerousness. But what more concrete help in determining sentencing can we glean from the review of known facts about patterns of juvenile sexual offending in chapter 3? The remainder of the analysis in this section follows that chapter in sorting juvenile sex offenders into three discrete classes: status offenders involved in consensual peer sex, first-time predatory offenders, and juvenile sexual recidivists.

Risk without Fault: Policy for Nonpredatory Peer Sex

The definition of delinquency in most states derives from the conduct prohibited by the various states' criminal codes. Under the California Welfare and Institutions Code § 602, for example, any minor within the jurisdiction of the court who commits a crime is for that reason delinquent. This statutory pattern generates an enormous potential volume of delinquent youths in those states in which laws defining statutory rape and indecent liberties with a child do not exclude conduct by young participants who are the same age and neither coerced nor deceived each other (see appendix A). With about half of all states not providing exclusions for peer sexual conduct, the number of consensual felonies committed in bedrooms and backseats by American adolescents numbers in the millions.

Appropriate policy toward juveniles involved in nonpredatory peer sex involves a mixture of the obvious with the not so obvious. The fourteen-year-old caught petting with a fourteen-year-old girlfriend should not be regarded as a felon in Idaho or anywhere else. This is yet another example of applying standards established for adults, where the sexual relations with youth involve exploitation, to age groups and social settings where exploitation cannot be so easily assumed. In this case, the felonization of adolescent sex is based on an invalid analogy with adult behavior and is an obvious candidate for reform.

But just as the sexual relations between two young adolescents should not be judged on the same basis as the sexual relationship between an adult and a child or young adolescent, it is also inappropriate to assume that sexual relations between two fourteen-year-olds should be regarded as equivalent to the consensual sex of two persons in their late twenties. The inexperience and lack of fully developed capacity that characterize early adolescent sexual conduct create special risks of pregnancy, disease, and emotional injury. The harms associated with peer sex among youths may be great, but there is no clear fault to be assigned as there is in cases involving a sexual predator. This combination of risk without fault is typical of a class of juvenile court issues that have a long and troublesome history—the status offenses and status offenders that have been an important and contentious part of juvenile justice since the court's beginning (Teitelbaum, 2002).

The easy part of reforming juvenile court policy toward nonpredatory peer sex is distinguishing such conduct from adolescent sexual conduct where there is culpability either because of the youth of the victim or the use of force by the offender. There is no fault basis for punishing either party to premature but consensual adolescent sex. The only good reason for intervention is to reduce the risks and harms associated with the conduct, but the track record of the juvenile courts in improving the lives of juvenile status offenders has been dismal.

The current system for responding to consensual teen sex in juvenile justice is deficient in both theory and practice. In all those jurisdictions that regard underage sex as criminal because the same prohibition that applies to adult behavior is deemed to apply to the young, this extension of liability is both silly and dangerous. The justification for adult punishment—the exploitation of the young—is missing from settings in which both participants are young. In practice, of course, the general prohibition of adolescent sex is ignored by families and law enforcement even in those jurisdictions that extend liability without regard to an offender's age. But the threat of prosecution is never a dead letter. Even if 99 percent of all discovered teen sex is not pushed into delinquency prosecution, the inappropriate prosecution of even a tiny minority of actors can produce a large number of unjust prosecutions (Caldwell, 2002). And the burden of unjust prosecution is probably more likely to fall on teens who are living in group homes or other forms of public custody where observed sexuality is more apt to be judged by legalistic standards. An institutional official is much more likely than mothers and fathers to call the police over teen petting. This means that kids already at very high risk are also in greater danger of prosecution for sexual acts that go unpunished for the vast majority of their peers.

Consensual adolescent and child sex should be decriminalized. But do such acts properly fall within the ambit of the juvenile court at all? The field of choice for adolescent sex between consenting peers is the same as for most of the other status offenses that have been a major battlefield for juvenile justice reform—either a drastic reduction in the coercive powers granted the juvenile courts or a removal of juvenile court jurisdiction altogether. The most frequent reform for status offenses during the generation after 1970 was the creation of a subdelinquent category of court jurisdiction—a minor in need of supervision—and the restructuring of court powers in such cases so that secure confinement could not be ordered. The net effect of this compromise—what is called "deinstitutionalization of status offenders"—is regarded as a positive but partial reform. Some juveniles can still end up in institutions because they have been "relabeled" as delinquents with drug, alcohol, or theft charges. The potential for relabeling of sex offenders is present when coercion is alleged. Other "relabled" adolescents end up in secure mental health facilities.

The alternative to deinstitutionalization of status offenders is the removal of these cases from the jurisdiction of juvenile courts altogether (see Institute of Judicial Administration, 1977). The potential for "relabeling" cases as delinquent sex charges or civil mental health cases would remain here as well, of course. But the juvenile court would be on record as opposed in principle to intervention in consensual sex cases, not because adolescents should be considered autonomous but rather because the only interventions available produce more harm than help (Zimring, 1982, chap. 5).

Either of the currently accepted paths for reforming status offender law would be an important improvement for jurisdictions that base delinquency on adult offenses such as indecent liberties or statutory rape. The "minor in need of supervision" approach with limits on confinement would probably be the path of least political resistance for reforms in most jurisdictions.

The Problem of Borderline Coercion

No matter what standard is adopted to govern noncoercive sexual conduct, there will be a substantial number of cases involving sexual conduct among peers and near peers in which social pressure was present and coercion is one plausible interpretation of what took place. Because of the huge number and variety of peer sexual encounters, authority figures may confront thousands of cases that are close to the border of problematic coercion. So any reform that diverts clear cases of consent will still leave a large number of cases in which the circumstances are ambiguous. These problem cases of borderline sexual delinquency are difficult both because accurate factfinding is often very problematic and also because appropriate sanctions are difficult to determine. Whatever progress is made in decriminalizing consensual juvenile sex, these "grey area" cases counsel that some margin of error is necessary in the juvenile court's punishment policy toward coercive sexual misconduct in the early and midteens.

A Rule for First Offenders

One important distinction in sentencing policy is between first-time culpable sexual offenders and repeat sexual offenders in the juvenile court. In light of what is currently known about sexual re-offending by first offenders, the best general rule for sentencing in first-offense cases is that, while considerations of current offense seriousness can result in punishment, *predictions of the offender's future sexual dangerousness should not play any independent role in determining either the duration of a penal sanction or its type.*

Excluding predictions of future dangerousness when sanctioning first-time sexual offenders is no guarantee of an easy decision or a lenient outcome. A highly serious offense involving an older teen offender might demand secure confinement whether or not considerations of future danger were incorporated into the sentencing process. And the intentional infliction of physical injury is an aggravating circumstance of significance without any reference to how it predicts future behavior. In short, sex offenders can be committed to reform schools or prisons for reasons that do not require predictions of future sex criminality.

The principal problem with clinical predictions that juvenile first-time sexual offenders are likely to commit future sex crimes is that there is *no* reliable actuarial basis for making such predictions. The standard follow-up three or four years after a first sexual-offense arrest reveals that less than one out of ten offenders commit another sex offense, often far less than one in ten. That these are not young persons skilled at evading detection can be seen by the much higher rates at which they are apprehended for other offenses (see chapter 3). There is no category of first-apprehension sex offender in adolescence with an expected recidivism rate as high as one in five.

The range of sanctions available for first offenders includes detention and even postadjudication incarceration for egregiously serious offenses, as well as counseling, victim empathy programs, and training in some social-sexual skills. But any aspect of sex-offender treatment or any adjunct to such treatment that is based either on assumptions of sexual deviance or on theories of sexual dangerousness is not justified. Secure confinement may in some cases be imposed as punishment but cannot be elected on the basis that secure treatment placements are justified by the sexual danger of the subject.

There are only two exceptions to the firewall that should be built between first-time offenders and presumptions of danger posed by them. Wherever a confirmed diagnosis of a sexual paraphilia is either pointed out by the juvenile's counsel or conceded by counsel in the litigation of the charge, treatment for deviant sexual tendencies can be a formal part of a juvenile court disposition. But even when paraphilia is the target of a treatment plan, there is usually no basis for concluding there is a high likelihood of future danger or for requiring noncommunity-based based treatment settings.

The only time a court can disregard a juvenile's status as a first-time sexual offender is when law enforcement authorities establish a pattern of multiple victimizations committed by the youth with different victims over a sustained period of time. Such an offender will have escaped prior detection despite predatory sexual encounters with a number of different victims. The evidence of a series of independent victimizations must be clear. That fact pattern when established by the criminal investigation process may be treated as the moral equivalent of recidivism, but the key features that distinguish such cases are misconduct over a long period of time as well as multiple victimizations. This does not happen often.

Will there be first-time offenders who clinical staff might regard as dangerous on other grounds who in fact will commit sex crimes after an initial processing in the juvenile justice system? Certainly. And forbidding the prediction of dangerousness in first-offender cases will prove to be a mistake in these cases. But a very large number of youths will be rescued from being falsely classified as sexual dangers for every dangerous first offender my approach would exclude from special dangerousness policies.

For most first-time sex offenders, the community's interest in their personal accountability and in safety can be met if the offender remains in a community setting. Reasonable conditions to minimize the potential for abuse (remember that ten-year-old J.G. in chapter 1 was restricted from unsupervised contacts with young children) do not imply heightened dangerousness on the part of the offender but rather are situational controls that need not carry public stigma. It should not require a prediction of special danger to ban thirteen- and fourteen-year-old boys from the unsupervised babysitting of younger children.

The general attitude of the juvenile justice system in cases of first-time offending should be to regard the sexual offense as wrongful, of course, but not as strong evidence of permanent pathology or fixed inclination. No other attitude can be sustained on the basis of present evidence; and thus any assumption of a link between first offenses and future dangerousness does not serve the interests of justice in juvenile courts.

Juvenile Sexual Recidivism

Repeat sexual offending after adjudication for a first-time sex offense is a background factor that increases the chances of future sex criminality and also provides evidence of sexual pathology, even in adolescents. But the reason that aggressive monitoring and other programmatic measures that seek to lower opportunities to re-offend can be justified in such cases is not solely statistical and predictive. In the policy framework outlined in this chapter, each juvenile offender identified as responsible for a second sexual offense would have already been tested with nonpredictive policies, and would have failed that test. The personal recidivism present on the record functions both as what Norval Morris calls an "anamnestic" prediction of future dangerousness (Morris, 1974) and as a failure to respond to less intensive supervision with appropriate restraint. Just as re-arrests when on probation are regarded as more blameworthy because they indicate abuse of less-intrusive sanctions, the failure to live up to a nonprediction of dangerousness justifies tighter levels of monitoring for the offender's second time through the system as a sex offender.

While juvenile sex re-offenders are a small minority of all juvenile sex criminals, they should not be regarded as in any sense a homogeneous group. Some forms of paraphilia such as exhibitionism have high rates of re-offending but exhibit low levels of social harm when not accompanied by more personally threatening deviant appetites. Some sexual recidivism may not indicate any long-term problems, since the re-arrest percentages for further offending are also not extraordinary. But the low base rate of sexual re-offense probably means that sex repeaters are less likely to be "adolescence limited" than adolescent re-arrests for property, status, or assault crimes that usually have much higher rates of recidivism. Recidivism in sex is so much less of a statistical likelihood than nondifferentiated delinquency that it is probably more predictive of pathology.

Yet given the heterogeneity among the re-offenders, and with no longitudinal studies that provide detailed sex-offense findings, decisionmakers cannot make convincing estimates of the factors associated with high risk, or judgments about the magnitudes of risk that different patterns of re-offense generate. Here is where the second set of studies advocated in the last section can provide much better guidance for future policy than any judge has at present. The first-time offender policies outlined above have a firmer basis in current statistical studies than *any* policy one might construct for groups of second-time sex offenders in juvenile court.

So the mix of motives that should inform the disposition of second-time sex offenders in juvenile court is importantly different from that for first-time offenders. The punishments or treatments designed for this group must still be deserved, and the policies favoring the prosecution of offending adolescents in juvenile rather than criminal courts are still important. The sanctioning decision for a juvenile second-time offender is a balance of multiple factors.

There is the further problem, however, that clinical predictions of juvenile sexual danger are frequently made with more confidence than the data properly permit. One reason for putting forward a prophylactic rule to ban predictions about the future conduct of a first-time offender is that the fear of future offenses tends to unfairly dominate the discourse on disposition. This is a genuine danger for second-time offenders as much as it is for first offenders, but the argument for excluding consideration of future risk in the former cases is much weaker. For juvenile recidivists, then, the challenge is to find a way of allowing discourse on the danger they pose to the community without it dominating the process of determining disposition of the case to an inappropriate degree.

One procedural safeguard in second-time offender cases could help discipline clinical evaluations of danger, and, because recidivist cases are infrequent even in large systems, the reform could be undertaken without much expense. This would involve the accused juvenile recidivist's being able to retain his own expert witness at court expense wherever a prediction of future dangerousness is likely to be an element in the prosecution. This would be especially important in cases where statistics on juvenile recidivism are insufficient for decisionmaking and where analogies drawn from adult sex-crime data are part of the prosecution's argument. If a prosecution expert is the only voice in court, the fairness of the proceeding is compromised. Providing the juvenile with resources to secure his own expert is the only effective way to produce a fair hearing on sexual danger in proceedings where that issue is of critical importance.

Special Issues for Sex Offenders in Juvenile Justice

Four special problems that arise in the treatment of sex cases in juvenile court require separate comment. Three of these concern distinctive practices in the treatment of sex offenders: the mix of past crimes investigation with treatment and supervision, the issue of therapist–patient privilege concerning disclosures in treatment, and the use of polygraph examinations as an adjunct to either the supervision or investigation of juvenile sex offenders. The fourth issue concerns the appropriateness of juvenile courts and the other institutions of juvenile justice for the treatment and sanctioning of sex offenders who have been appropriately diagnosed as sexually deviant and with a history of expressing deviant impulses in serious criminal conduct.

Investigation, Supervision, and Treatment

In theory the investigation of criminal offenses, the supervision of juvenile offenders, and the clinical treatment of young persons for conduct disorders are three separate functions carried out by workers trained in the three respective professions. But both the developing practice of juvenile sex-offender treatment and the traditional structure of juvenile probation have encouraged combining at least some of these functions as part of the duties of a single professional. Indeed, the 1993 National Task Force report we considered in chapter 4 recommends the treatment staff member be responsible for all three functions. Although the treatment professional is never a full-fledged police investigator—she is not given a set of unsolved cases by the police and asked to find guilty parties—evidently all sex offenses that might have been committed by the treatment client are an investigatory target of the treatment process. Whether and how often the investigatory ambitions of treatment staff lead to prosecution is not reported in the Task Force document, nor anywhere else. In addition, the 1993 report proposes that the treatment professional take the lead role in supervising the activities of the offender in the community or in the institution, and also design and administer treatment.

While the National Task Force model of the sex-offender treatment professional involves a combination of all three roles, the usual pattern for juvenile court probation staff and youth treatment programs is to combine two of the functions—treatment and supervision—without the third function of criminal investigation. The probation officer checks up on her juvenile charge with a relentless energy that the juvenile offender might regard as totalitarian, and what the probation staff learns about the juvenile's current life—school attendance, friends, and recreation—contributes to the assessment of the youth's current status and to treatment planning.

But there are problems that can arise in combining professional functions within the juvenile justice system. Different roles expected of the same person can result in conflicted priorities or loyalties. The classic instance of such conflicts in an adversarial system is having the same person function as both prosecutor and judge. The prosecutor is expected to prove guilt and push for punishment, while the judge is expected initially to be neutral as to the defendant's guilt and the level of punishment to be meted out, if any. How can the same person be expected to carry out both functions?

Does combining the functions of supervision and treatment of juvenile offenders in the same person produce a similar conflict? In the case of juvenile probation, the standard answer to that question is no, but the issue is not free from doubt. Supervising a juvenile requires asking lots of questions about current behavior and carefully scrutinizing the answers. Remaining skeptical about much of the accounts provided by adolescents in response to specific questions is an inevitable part of supervision. While the supervisory tone frequently can become confrontational with resistive adolescents, this is not regarded as inconsistent with the treatment process because adequate information concerning the juvenile's current activities is important for treatment and because the supervisor's commitment to the youth's welfare is assumed.

Combining the responsibility for supervision and treatment has never posed a serious problem in the design of the juvenile justice system because juvenile courts are modeled on the parental function. Parents, after all, are expected to undertake the combined functions of supervision, instruction, and remediation of their children's behavior. Parental supervision and remediation are not regarded as conflicting functions because of the commitment to the child's welfare that is the essential feature of our conception of the parental role. As long as a parental commitment to treatment and supervision is efficiently combined in the same person with a clear dedication to the child's welfare, the supervisory role does not compromise treatment.

This assumption that parents have their children's best welfare at heart is not, however, so easily made in the case of juvenile court probation. If the punishments threatened by the court for failure in supervision include some that do not take much account of the offender's interests, the analogy with parental roles does not hold. Similarly, if the information produced by supervisory functions can be used to the manifest disadvantage of the subject, then a conflict of roles may be anticipated.

The problems that result from making the same professional into a criminal investigator as well as supervisor as well as therapist are considerable. Adding pressure for criminal detection to the load is the brick that breaks the camel's back. If much of the time and energy invested by a treatment professional in a therapeutic relationship is spent trying to discover whether the person being treated has committed other offenses and, if so, then arranging for further prosecution, the offender will only be motivated to deceive or not cooperate with the investigator-cum-therapist.

While some may argue for the presumed efficiency of having one therapist function as both a cop and clinician for the juvenile court, the adversarial nature of the law enforcement role clearly poses too great a potential for conflict. Even if it is appropriate to keep juvenile sex offenders under continual scrutiny for crimes they might have committed prior to the court's referral to treatment, such investigation should be conducted by persons who are not in charge of treatment and supervision. All these tasks might be carried out in the same institutional setting, but no good case can be made that they should all be the responsibility of the same person.

Nor is there any obvious justification in the available literature for spending substantial resources and efforts in the attempt to discover past illegal conduct of those young sex offenders who are already being treated and subjected to community supervision. The sex-treatment professional is not regarded as a criminal investigator by the police and does not have a list of important unsolved crimes she is expected to investigate. Moreover, it is not clear that the facts about previous conduct discovered in this manner are important to law enforcement. There are no indications in the literature that police agencies place great emphasis on the benefits they gain from treatment staff detection.

What, then, is the value of trying to use the treatment process as a path to additional prosecution? Since the offender is already in treatment, his identification has already been achieved. What does a second conviction for a past act add to the value of the adjudication process as a control on present and future conduct? If this is a first conviction, there will be little of predictive value in prior acts unless they constitute a long list of offending behavior over a substantial time. If the real reason for discovering past acts is only for the proper diagnosis and classification of the treatment subject, the effort to prosecute for past conduct does not add any value to these treatment goals but creates an additional incentive for nondisclosure on the parts of the juvenile sex offender and his lawyer. How does the willingness of the therapist to initiate prosecution for past acts assist in the construction of an accurate case history? And if it does not, why isn't the supervision and treatment process better served when the therapist does not fill the additional role of criminal investigator?

While the National Task Force has argued for an investigative role for the therapist, the specific issues that we have seen to be involved in a combination of functions were not recognized in 1993 report, nor were any specific advantages of prosecution-oriented investigation ever mentioned. It was instead assumed that the community would benefit in unspecified ways from a maximum rate of prosecutions. Once that had been assumed, the search for prosecutable crimes in a treatment subject's past was evidently recommended as a way to prove the therapist's loyalty to certain community interests—namely, the reprosecution of a juvenile offender who is already in treatment and has only a low likelihood of sexual recidivism. But why? And should the therapist also alert prosecutors to any burglaries, drug offenses, or car thefts in the personal histories of their patients?

It is hard to have a contextual understanding of the impact of combining criminal investigation with sex-offender treatment because it is not clear what the therapist's attitude toward the patient should be in that setting. If there is value in a sex offender's trust and confidence in the therapist, the potential for conflict that arises from the attempt to use treatment data to secure grounds for further prosecution seems obvious.

Therapist–Patient Privilege in Juvenile Sex-Offender Treatment

One hazard of the clinical treatment of persons who manifest antisocial tendencies concerns the therapist's duties to his patients and to the community when indications of future dangerous or criminal activity emerge in the course of treatment. Both the canons of professional ethics for therapists and the legal rules of evidence confer a qualified privilege on confidential communications between patient and therapist, as is also expected in the relationship between clergy and their parishioners and lawyers and their clients. The usual privilege is "qualified" because the law does not wish to allow the plans for future dangerous or criminal acts to be discussed with impunity in a therapeutic relationship. Privilege, then, does not extend to communications regarding future acts, and the duty to warn victims may be imposed by tort law in such cases (see, e.g., *Tarasoff v. Regents of the University of California*, 131 Cal. Rptr. 14 [1976]).

But why not also require the therapist to reveal information about past criminal acts? One way of viewing the privilege about past conduct is as a cost–benefit calculation made by policymakers that the positive impact of confidentiality in treatment better serves the general welfare of society than any aid to law enforcement that might come from therapists' passing along information they obtain about past criminal acts. The client's trust engendered by privileged communication in the therapeutic setting is regarded as an investment in the greater capacity of the treatment process to protect society from future offenses. Although the patient is not granted any immunity from prosecution for those offenses he reveals in the course of therapy, the state cannot use the process of therapy as a tool for criminal discovery.

Is there any reason to doubt the wisdom of this balance in the specific setting of juvenile sex offenders? While the National Task Force rejects the idea of any privilege between therapist and client, it does not respond to any of the arguments in favor of this privilege nor any regarding the costs of its abolition. Instead, it appears to use the issue of privilege as a way of determining who identifies with offenders (supporters of privilege) and who with the interests of community protection (those who would abolish privilege). Having created such a simplistic status competition, the Task Force chooses the community.

Yet one question not addressed in all this is whether the trust that can be established when treatment takes place in a setting of confidentiality might actually serve community interests better than the law enforcement gains that nonprivileged communication between therapist and client might produce.

Whatever the correct approach to the issue of privilege, the same set of conclusions should apply to patients who receive therapy as part of their treatment for having committed theft, life-threatening assault, and sex offenses. In areas of special legislative priority such as child abuse, the presence or absence of privilege should be the same for nonsexual offenders in treatment as for sex offenders. The way in which policies toward sex offenders and those who treat them have been addressed in isolation from the policies that apply in other areas of clinical treatment and law enforcement is a warning sign not only of inconsistency in policy but of questionable decisionmaking about juvenile and adult sex offenders.

It has yet to be conclusively shown that protecting disclosures made during the treatment process of past sex criminality would in any substantial way undermine the interests of law enforcement. Under those circumstances a qualified privilege similar to that in the practice of medicine and clinical psychology might better serve both the interests in the prevention of recidivism for those sex offenders who are appropriate candidates for treatment, and the integrity of the treatment process itself.

The Polygraph

The third procedure that sets some types of juvenile sex-offender treatment apart from other juvenile court matters is the polygraph. The Juvenile Sex Offender Task Force reported that 24 percent of the more than 800 programs that treat juvenile offenders use polygraph examinations (National Adolescent Perpetrator Network, 1993, p. 85). How often such examinations are used and with what results are not known. But the practice again illustrates the separateness of juvenile sex-offender policy from the policies used for other types of juvenile offenders, and the tension in juvenile sex-offender treatment between therapeutic and adversarial orientations.

The polygraph or lie detector is designed to chart a human subject's physiological responses during question-and-answer sessions. The pattern of those responses is then interpreted by an "operator" as evidence of whether, when responding to a particular question, the subject is more likely to have told the truth or to have lied (National Research Council, 2003). The strategy of lie detection is really twofold: first, by persuading the subject that the machine can discover attempts at deception, the operator can coerce the subject into truth telling; second, if this interrogation effect does not happen, the operator can then fall back on using physiological responses during the examination as evidence of false statements. So lie detectors are in the first instance an interrogation technique.

The career of lie detection over more than seven decades has been a mixed one. The results of polygraph examinations are not admissible in court as evidence of the truth or falsity of answers provided to polygraph operators because the legal system does not regard them as a scientifically accurate measure of veracity. But private security firms, police, and intelligence agencies use polygraph interrogation by licensed operators as part of security screening and investigation work. One reason for the contrast between the scientific reputation of the polygraph and its frequent use in screening and interrogation is its value as a method of inducing truth telling from fearful subjects. This is a powerful tool that would greatly assist the interrogator even if the physiological data were useless (National Research Council, 2003). All that is required is the subject's worry that the procedure may be accurate.

It is not known whether the 168 juvenile sex-offender treatment programs that report use of polygraphs employ them as a typical or an exceptional intervention. Their original use in juvenile sex cases probably derived from their application to adult sex offenders, where the polygraph is a method for conducting interrogations about past acts, for supervision purposes, and for making recommendations about sanctions and treatment programs. The polygraph is believed to be useful in this setting because it increases the volume of behaviors that sex offenders acknowledge committing (see Colorado Department of Public Safety, 2000). Moreover, it is believed to be necessary for those adult sex offenders who are skilled at deception.

The claims for the special usefulness and in some cases the necessity for polygraph testing of adult sex offenders is an important issue because polygraph examinations are not a standard part of probation or supervision for any other group of adult criminal offenders. Is this skill at deception on the part of adult sex offenders shared by juvenile sex offenders? Should the juvenile sex offender be compared to the juvenile armed robber, drive-by shooter, burglar, and vandal—none of whom are subject to interrogations with polygraphs—or to the adult sexual offender? To be sure, juvenile sex offenders attempt to minimize their previous criminal deeds in exchanges with authority figures, but so do the great majority of other delinquents.

This is not the place for a sustained analysis of the pros and cons of polygraphs in dealing with juvenile sex offenses, but three points need to be made here about how current policy has evolved on this question. The first point is that polygraph examination is an interrogation technique that is usually the task of a specialist operator who is not part of any therapeutic team (Hunter & Lexier, 1998). If the polygraph is needed at all in the juvenile sex-offense context, it can just as easily be performed as an adjunct to probation supervision or criminal prosecution as in any treatment setting. So any use of this interrogation strategy should not be considered as part of a treatment plan. Clinical staff can evaluate the reports that polygraphers make, but the technique has the same relationship to behavioral therapy as a fingerprint kit or a security camera.

The second point is that any principled analysis of the promise and problems of lie detection as a supervision strategy for juvenile offenders should consider a wide range of juvenile offenders. Chapter 3 showed that juvenile offenders who commit nonsexual assaults and robberies are a much greater threat to the life and safety of other children than the juvenile sex offender. The juvenile sex offender—who accounts for almost one in every five sex arrests but only about one in every twenty sex homicides—is not obviously skilled in evading detection in the manner of the serial pedophile. So the rationale for polygraphy for *any* class of juvenile offender has yet to be demonstrated.

There are other issues as well. Are the deceptions required by operators for successful polygraph interrogations problematic as an intentional policy of a juvenile court (Hunter & Lexier, 1998)? Should there be special limits on the abuse of truth and use of coercion with minors? How great must the supervisional and investigative need be before this special procedure is introduced?

The third point that must be made about lie detectors is that none of the questions just raised have ever been asked or answered within the juvenile justice system. Whatever else the current practice of polygraph examinations on juvenile sex offenders might be, it is fundamentally lawless. The implicit assumption that has created the downward drift of lie-detection-aided interrogation of juveniles is that any practice that is appropriate for adult sex offenders must also be appropriate for juveniles. So here again the false analogy between very different types of offenders and offenses is the only justification of existing policy and practice.

Sexual Deviants in Juvenile Courts

The final special issue I want to raise regarding sex offenders in the juvenile justice system is more fundamental than the procedural problems just discussed. The question is whether there is any category of sex offender within the customary ages of juvenile court jurisdiction who should be regarded as unsuitable for the juvenile court because of the threat he poses for future sexual dangerousness. The answer depends on what sort of broader social policies are in place to control those identified as sexual deviants and to protect the community. Any policy in the case of an adolescent sex offender that seeks a combination of treatment and the offender's opportunity to live a normal adult life would be more easily administered by juvenile than by criminal court. But if, under a different policy scheme, long custodial sentences and permanent stigma are used as control measures for any class of adolescent sex offender, then waiver to the criminal court might be appropriate as a precondition to these policies that willingly sacrifice the interests of the offenders.

The overwhelming majority of juvenile sex offenders are not diagnosable sexual deviants at any point prior to aging out of the juvenile system. In juvenile justice systems that extend jurisdiction until the eighteenth birthday, however, there will be some offenders who possess both documented sexual recidivism after treatment and community supervision and who display clinical indications of sexual paraphilia. Until the studies urged in the first part of this chapter are completed, it will not be known whether this group numbers in the hundreds or the thousands, but no one would deny the importance of designing appropriate policy for persistent sexual offenders. And yet the question remains: Do they belong in juvenile or criminal courts?

Even if the number of identified sexual deviants is small, it is a group with extraordinary heterogeneity. Young sex offenders with documented histories of sadism are a distinct problem. Flexner and Baldwin were careful to mention their special concern for offenders who manifest "sex viciousness" more than eighty years ago (Flexner & Baldwin, 1916, p. 78). By contrast, the adolescent with only a fetishistic orientation will be a far less problematic criminal threat, with theft of clothing being the most likely offense and no fixed need for criminal offenses to express his sexual needs. The behavior of an adolescent with exhibitionist patterns will reveal a closer link between his sexual orientation and criminal activity, but the offenses do not usually involve contact with victims. It is also possible, of course, that noncontact sexual deviations can be combined with other deviant tendencies more likely to result in contact offenses.

While a large number of juvenile sex arrests are for offenses that involve very young victims, it is unlikely that many juvenile offenders with child victims can be diagnosed with confidence as pedophiles. Most of the young victim cases are opportunistic and do not involve diagnosable psychological abnormalities. The DSM-IV-R prohibition on basing a diagnosis of pedophilia on behavior that occurs before the offender is sixteen will also keep the population of confirmed juvenile justice system pedophiles disproportionately low. It is, therefore, more than possible that the easily classified adolescent sexual deviants might tend to commit the noncontact offenses that are regarded as the least serious of common sex crimes.

What might argue against a juvenile court disposition for charges against deviant sexual recidivists is neither a high re-arrest rate for this group of offenders nor the lack of appropriate treatment options available in the juvenile system. The re-arrest rates of many groups of juvenile delinquents are in fact higher than those reported for sex offenders (see Wolfgang, Figlio, & Sellin, 1972). And the availability of treatment programs in the juvenile system is, by reputation, better than in the criminal justice system (see, e.g., National Adolescent Perpetrator Network, 1993, p. 20). But public opinion may demand interventions to control deviant sex offenders that carry larger restrictions of liberty than the juvenile courts can impose without violating their commitment to fostering the healthy development of delinquents.

In many of the most serious sex offenses—forcible rapes with intentional and serious injury—waiver to criminal court is appropriate because the minimum punishment the community will tolerate exceeds the maximum punishment that juvenile courts properly are empowered to impose.

For crimes such as these, the waiver standard for sex offenders would not be different than for juveniles charged with life-threatening violence (see Zimring, 2000).

But there are also offenses in the middle range of seriousness that do not require confinement of extraordinary length or substantial prejudice to the opportunity of the juvenile to experience a nearly normal transition to adulthood, but in which categorical judgments about sex offenders and future dangerousness do push for longer incarceration and permanent stigma. When drastic sanctions are imposed, the quality of legal representation and other procedural protections available in juvenile courts will often seem inadequate, and the drastic consequences that a juvenile court would have to administer might create a tension with the commitment of that court to the future prospects of juvenile offenders. When extreme sanctions are required of the juvenile court by legislative fiat, or when the court itself concludes that the danger of some categories of adolescent sex offenders demands responses that compromise the developmental needs and future prospects of the delinquent, the waiver of such cases to criminal courts might protect the juvenile court from compromising its mission.

Channeling adolescent sex offenders into criminal courts, however, might expose them to even greater prejudice than they would face before a juvenile court that is compromised in the way just described. To the extent that a juvenile court setting softens the sharp edges of a sex-offender policy dominated by concerns about offender dangerousness, the individual youth may always prefer the juvenile to the criminal court. But the coherence of the court as an institution and its ability to observe limits in its punishment of other delinquents may suffer if severe sex-offender regimes are kept within juvenile justice. In this way, the interests of juvenile sex offenders may be opposed to the interests of other delinquents and of the court as an institution.

This conflict can be avoided if criminal courts were to recognize the developmental aspects of adolescent sex offenders as well as the findings that demonstrate their diminished culpability. If the criminal courts were also sensitive to the special status of adolescent offenders, waiver to criminal court would not necessarily disserve the defendant. But the pressures toward unqualified punitive orientations in criminal courts have been quite powerful in recent years, and there is evidence that juvenile courts have resisted the pressure for increased incarceration more than have criminal courts (Zimring, 2002, figure 1). If the political environment of criminal courts for policy toward sex offenders were to moderate, the pressure on juvenile courts to overpredict the dangers to the community posed by adolescent sex offenders might also abate. But until the climate of opinion moderates, students of juvenile justice policy must be prepared to recognize and make hard choices relating to the disposition of adolescent sex offenders.

There are two oddly contrasting truths about current knowledge of adolescent sexual misconduct and its control. In the first place, there are basic information gaps in our understanding of the nature of the behaviors, their causes, and the significance of current behavior as a prediction of future orientation and conduct. The unknown parameters of adolescent sexual misconduct are inexcusable. That said, however, it is also true that we know much better than we do. The distinctive features and prognoses of adolescent sex offenses have been documented for sixty years, but there is a chronic failure to fully appreciate the singular nature of sexual offending by children and youth. The false premise of much current policy is the easy analogy drawn between adolescent and adult sexual criminality. No policy that relies on such a misapprehension can effectively serve either justice or public safety.

Chapter 7

Registration, Community Notification, and Juvenile Sex Offenders: Resolving Policy Conflicts

The systematic registration and public notification of [juvenile sex offenders] may be unwarranted and unnecessary.

—*Lisa Trivits and N. Dickon Reppucci, "Application of Megan's Law to Juveniles,"* American Psychologist *(2002)*

The major changes in policy toward sex offenders in recent years have concerned not the definition of offenses but rather the consequences of conviction. The first major shift was in the number of persons incarcerated for sex crimes other than forcible rape, which grew more than sevenfold during the seventeen years after 1980. This increased use of prison terms for sex offenders was part of a much broader shift toward greater use of prison sentences for serious crimes. Over the twenty-nine years after 1972, the prison population in the United States expanded sevenfold, from 203,000 in 1972 to 1.4 million in 2001 (Bureau of Justice Statistics, 2002). Those incarcerated as part of this trend were convicted for a wide variety of offenses. While the growth of incarceration for sex crimes in the 1980s and 1990s was particularly sharp, it was part of a general trend.

The second wave of changes in policy toward sex offenders involved a set of statutory enactments directed specifically at those convicted of sex crimes. Legislation during the 1980s and 1990s created civil commitment statutes that effectively could continue the secure confinement of those classified as sexually dangerous after their criminal prison sentences had been served (see *Kansas v. Hendricks,* 521 U.S. 346 [1997]). By the mid-1990s, seventeen states had some form of such a civil commitment law (Alexander, 1999). Other legislation specially directed at sex offenders permitted the use of chemical agents to inhibit sexual arousal and erections, referred to as "chemical castration."

But the most widespread statutory reform of the 1990s was the creation of special requirements of registration for persons convicted of particular sex offenses (and some other offenses if children were victims). For some classes of offenders, this can require that citizens and school officials be notified of the identity, address, and employment of sex offenders living or working in the community. Since the mid-1990s, state registration and notification laws have been required for state anticrime programs to receive federal funding. By 1997, all fifty states had passed some form of such laws. Twelve years earlier, only five states required sex-offender registration and there were no community notification laws anywhere (Garfinkle, 2003).

This chapter examines the operations and rationale for registration and community notification laws as they relate to juvenile sex offenders. The first section distinguishes between registration and notification as sex-crime prevention strategies, and explores the assumptions about sex offenders that underlie their being singled for registration and notification. In the second section, I provide a profile of the treatment of juvenile offenders under different regimes of state notification and registration statutes. The next section contrasts the assumptions about offenders embedded in current registration and notification laws with the understanding of young offenders that informs the policies of most juvenile courts. Then, in the chapter's final section, I discuss appropriate policy toward juvenile sex offenders in state registration and notification systems, and consider the options available to juvenile courts when such systems contradict policies the courts deem to be important.

The Structure of Sex-Offender Registration and Notification

The state systems legislated in the 1990s are a mix of two different methods for identifying persons previously convicted of sex crimes in order to prevent or to help investigate other sex offenses. A *registration* requirement imposes a duty on a sex offender to make himself known to the police in the community where he wishes to reside. This duty to register provides the police with a list of previously convicted sex offenders and the crimes for which they were convicted, information that is presumed to be useful when a new sex offense is reported. The records of all registered offenders can be compared with the fact pattern of the new case, and offenders with similar offense histories can become targets of the current investigation, particularly if they live or work close to the scene of the crime. This venerable law enforcement technique was immortalized in the 1942 film *Casablanca* when the police chief orders his officers to "round up the usual suspects." Sex-offender registration provides the police with a list of the usual suspects.

The crime-prevention potential of registration provisions might also extend to deterring those offenders with previous records from new acts of sexual misconduct, because they know that the authorities can link any future crime to their known prior conduct, but this has never been rigorously tested. Registration certainly provides an additional step to the routine investigation of sex offenses. To the extent that particular types of sex crime are usually committed by a small segment of the population and offenders repeatedly target the same type of victim for the same sexual contact, the registration lists might be a helpful part of the investigation process. But if there is no strong tendency of offenders to repeat the same patterns of sex crime, and if other members of the community might be tempted to commit the sexual behavior that is the core of the current offense, then the list of prior sex offenders will prove less efficient in solving new offenses.

Where registration requirements exist, they also give the police a criminal charge that can be used whenever persons under a duty to register fail to do so. Where police suspect an unregistered felon of further wrongdoing but lack proof, the failure-to-register charge provides a ready criminal charge that can be an alternative route to further criminal conviction.

Registration systems for felons or for sex offenders have some precedent in the United States, and offender registration schemes are also a part of law enforcement in other countries. In France, for example, broad citizen registration with the police is standard (Bertillon, 1889; Harling, 1996). Until recently, however, sex-offender registration was not common in the United States.

The second method for identifying persons convicted of sex offenses comprises the *community notification* systems. These systems, which proliferated in the 1990s in state laws and that were mandated in federal legislation, have no true precedent in modern law enforcement, although public notice and warning about offenders have been used sporadically for centuries. The so-called Megan's Laws rest on the belief that it is possible for potential victims, their families, and community institutions to protect themselves against known sexual threats. Megan Kanka was a young girl murdered by a sex offender previously in prison. The family of the original Megan thought that knowledge that a child molester lived in the neighborhood could have generated preventative actions by her household.

As used in the various new state laws, community notification is a supplement to registration requirements rather than an alternative to them, so any benefits that might come from registration may also be expected in communities that add the notification requirement. But how much additional prevention actually comes from notification? When parents of potential victims learn about the presence in the community of a convicted sex offender, they can of course move to what they consider to be safer locations, and schools and day-care facilities might also prohibit known sex felons with child victims from being on their premises. But why should a law-abiding family have to flee a community to be safe from predatory sex crime? And is teaching seven- and eight-year-old children to stay away from certain men a more effective tool than teaching them not to trust any strange men?

If notification schemes were not ubiquitous, those states that had such systems could also benefit from sex offenders' moving to other jurisdictions in which notification is not required. When every state has such a law, however, a basic community notification system will not drive out offenders since they have nowhere to go to escape its requirements. In this sense, the preventive goals of notification laws are victims of the success of the genre.

The extent to which any potential victims and child-serving institutions actively respond to community notification, and the effects that has on rates of victimization, are not known. There has yet to be careful research concerning the effectiveness of community notification in preventing sex crimes. One natural limit on the preventive impact of community notification is that previously convicted sex offenders are by no means the largest threat to potential victims of forcible rape, child molestation, and forcible fondling. With very high volumes of several forms of sex offenses projected from victim surveys, and with social acquaintances and family frequently involved as offenders, any prevention that targets only a small proportion of the sex-offender population will not provide anything near comprehensive safety to potential victims (Lynch, 1999; Russell, 1982; U.S. Department of Health and Human Services, 2003).

The lack of discussion concerning the effectiveness of community notification as a preventive measure results from two political themes that emerged from the crime policy debates of the 1990s—themes that had more to do with the architecture of community notification than with its efficacy as crime prevention. The first major theme was distrust of government (see Zimring, Hawkins, & Kamin, 2001, chap. 11). The 1990s was a period when anger at the ineffectiveness of governmental crime control was a major feature of political debate. The effectiveness of registration alone as a preventive measure depends on the efficiency and the sincerity of police officials, and was for that reason suspect during the mid-1990s.

Community notification, however, has one very attractive feature for an age when both the intentions and the capacity of governments are in doubt: it is a mechanism that (once the notifications are made) does not depend for its operation on the government. The antigovernment rhetoric of citizen notification thus fit the mood of the era in which Megan's Laws were created. And that was one reason for assuming the crime-preventive potential of the policy.

A second feature of community notification that made it popular even if its preventive potential went unresearched was the obvious additional harm that community notification would impose on sex offenders when they were exposed. A curious feature of the 1990s crime-control debate has been called the "zero-sum fallacy," which held that anything that hurts criminal offenders must to the same extent also help crime victims (Zimring, Hawkins, & Kamin, 2001, chap. 11). When such rhetoric is appealing, then the obvious stigma, isolation, and public shaming of sex offenders by community notification would seem like a promising strategy, even if the mechanics of exactly how it would help potential victims were not fully developed. The further punishment of sex offenders was attractive for its own sake for those who resented sex offenders, and it also promised results to those who believed that anything which created substantial disadvantage to offenders must also help their potential victims.

So the mechanics of sex-offender notification fit the rhetoric of the debate about crime and crime prevention during the mid-1990s. In this way, while the provisions of Megan's Laws were specific to sex crimes involving children, the political forces that shaped these laws and that have protected them from scrutiny were a product of the broader distrust of government effectiveness and the belief that punishing sex offenders directly correlates with benefiting their victims.

Registration and Notification Laws and the Juvenile Sex Offender

The juvenile sex offender was not a high priority in the registration and notification legislation that swept across the country in the 1990s. The federal laws that set standards for state registration and notification neither require nor prohibit the application of those statutes to juveniles (U.S. Department of Justice, 1999). As a result, the fifty state laws differ widely in whether and how juveniles are treated under registration and notification systems. One commentator reports that in thirty-eight states systems of registration and notification covering juveniles are in effect, implying they are absent in only twelve states (Caldwell, 2002).

Even where offenses adjudicated in juvenile courts are excluded from these systems, offenders under the usual statutory age for criminal court can still be included in mandatory registration and notification when tried and convicted in the criminal court. At the other end of the spectrum are states that do not distinguish between juvenile and criminal courts or offenders, and hence the statutes governing registration and notification of sex offenders apply equally to all. The policies in most states fall somewhere in between. Some provide separate registries for juveniles and adult offenders, with separate rules governing when and how offenders can leave the registration system. This is the pattern in the Idaho law discussed in chapter 1. Other states have only one registry, but separate rules have been developed by courts or administrative agencies for juveniles as a class or for younger subsets of juvenile offenders. This is the situation in New Jersey since that state's Supreme Court decision in *In re Registrant J.G.*, 777 A.2d 891 (2001), discussed in chapter 1. In some jurisdictions, registration is required for juvenile offenders, but not community notification.

Not only is there a wide variation in state policies toward juveniles, but the legislative intent among the statutes is often so unclear that the same language can be interpreted in opposite ways—as requiring registration and notification or not. In her analysis of state Megan's Laws, Elizabeth Garfinkle (2003) reports that the laws in eighteen jurisdictions are silent on the question of juvenile court adjudications and juvenile offenders. Does this mean the juvenile courts and young offenders in those jurisdictions do not fall within the purview of registration and notification sanctions, or that all sex offenders regardless of age are covered? Courts can interpret legislative silence both ways. While exclusion would seem the most sensible approach to a statute that does not mention juveniles, other commentaries that count thirty-eight states now extend coverage to juveniles, which would include at least six of the laws with no reference to juveniles (Caldwell, 2002).

A review of the available public records that document the legislative processes in enacting registration and notification systems produces one clear finding: no consideration of empirical data nor sustained policy analysis concerning the costs and benefits of different models of inclusion or exclusion of juveniles was undertaken by either the U.S. Congress or any of the fifty states. The wave of Megan's Laws that crested in the mid-1990s were not models of careful and well-researched statutory draftsmanship on any topics, and the special circumstances of juvenile courts and juvenile offenders were of only peripheral concern.

The wide variation in policy toward juvenile offenders under registration and notification laws provides a natural opportunity to test whether variations in Megan's Law policies toward juveniles had any influence on the behavior of juvenile courts and on juvenile offenders. Are juveniles in those states mandating they be fully covered by registration and notification sanctions responsible for the same proportion of sex-crime charges or for a smaller proportion of total arrests for rape and other sex offenses? Do juveniles in these same states have lower or higher rates of sex-offense recidivism than in states not requiring registration and notification of juvenile offenders? Is the ratio of juvenile sex arrests to sex-crime adjudications higher in those jurisdictions where adjudication involves the registration and notification systems? How often do families of juvenile offenders who are covered by those systems move to jurisdictions where they are not covered? To date, there have been no attempts to measure the consequences of policy variation along these lines.

The same low priority generally accorded policies of juvenile registration and notification also likely explains the low degree of legislative change in state policy. While the cross-sectional variation in Megan's Law coverage of juveniles is wide, there have not been extensive rethinking over time once such policies are in place. It appears that the extent of juvenile sanctioning is a relatively unimportant detail in the pattern of registration and notification laws, and there is little apparent pressure to evaluate or to reform it. When changes do occur, however, they can be as dramatic as Illinois's explicit extension of registration and notification sanctions to juvenile offenders, which evidently now extends lifetime registration requirements to twelve-year-olds with certain juvenile adjudication records (*In re J. W., a Minor*, WL 369679 ([Ill. 2003]).

Nor is there any extensive record of analyzing the costs and benefits of juvenile inclusion. While it is easy to consider the contest between child victims and adult sex offenders as involving discrete populations, the issue of juvenile sex-offender registration and notification would seem to involve the interest of minor children on both sides of the ledger. How many children and youth who violated the law once but would not do so again even without notification should have their interests sacrificed to prevent one potential sex-crime victim from becoming an actual victim? When conceived as a competition between victims and adult offenders, the number of criminals the public would be willing to handicap for a single case of prevention would be very high indeed. Would that balance-of-harms analysis change when children and youth are at risk on both sides of the equation? Should it change?

If there is little or no evidence of *any* crime prevention from notification schemes, should the fact that the offenders are themselves children and adolescents weigh against the ordinary citizen's willingness to support as a public good practices that injure such offenders? If there is some need for crime prevention benefit to offset the harm to young offenders that registration and notification produce, where is the burden of proof to lie in evaluating the evidence of benefit and cost?

In the short and confused history of registration and notification laws, these sorts of questions have not been answered. Indeed, they have not been asked. The final two sections of this chapter recommend a specific policy analysis for use by legislators and court officials who must make decisions about the application of registration and notification to juvenile sex offenders.

Policies in Conflict

There is a fundamental conflict between the view of juvenile offenders that animates policy in U.S. juvenile courts and the view of sex offenders that underlies the assumptions and policy choices of Megan's Laws. The juvenile court regards the delinquent as neither fully mature nor set in his ways, but rather as a changeable and to some extent malleable entity. By contrast, the image of the sex offender subject to community notification laws is that of a person with a permanent identity as one who poses a sexual threat to the community, who has a set of fixed preferences in victims, and who is driven by all-but-inevitable urge to recidivate.

What distinguishes these two views is not just different moral judgments about the blameworthiness of juveniles for previous criminal conduct, but also different assumptions about the future conduct of convicted sex offenders. Because these conflicting views rely on behavioral traits that have been studied, it is possible to make some judgments about which outlook better fits with the results of research. In this section I provide some foundation for distinguishing false from true conflicts, and then turn in the final section to explore the pertinent available data on juvenile sex offenders.

False versus True Conflicts

The underlying ideology of the U.S. juvenile court is not to any substantial extent directed specifically to the problems of adjudicating youthful sex offenders. As chapter 5 demonstrated, some violent sex offenders are waived to criminal courts because of the seriousness of the offenses committed. The juvenile court judge who confronts an adolescent fitting the offender stereotype that inspired the passage of notification laws—a dangerous, pathological, specialized, and potentially violent sexual recidivist—would in all likelihood favor registration and notification in such a case. But in most systems, that type of defendant would also be transferred to criminal court. There is no conflict of values in the disposition of such cases, but they do not stay in the juvenile system.

But what about the case involving a juvenile offender who at age fourteen was attempting to have sexual intercourse with an eight- or nine-year-old girl and who presents a 4–9 percent chance of re-arrest for sexual crime in the next five years? For this kind of case, the juvenile court would probably oppose public notification and the consequent long-term labeling that would result. And if a registration and notification sanction applied by statute, the result would be a true conflict between the policy preferences of juvenile courts and those that are at least implicitly expressed by the statute. To put it differently, a true conflict exists when the two systems—juvenile court and state registration and notification law—would favor different outcomes for the same juvenile. In most juvenile sex cases, long-term registration and any public notification are in clear conflict with juvenile court policy preferences. I later argue that when juvenile courts confront true conflicts between the policies they hold to be of fundamental importance and statutory policy, they are free to use lawful means to advance the policies they favor. (For a civil law analysis of interstate conflicts of policy that reaches a similar conclusion in inter-state conflicts, see Currie, 1963.)

Fact versus Value

Where true conflicts between statutory registration and notification policies and those of juvenile courts exist, it is often difficult to tell whether the divergence in desired outcome results more from different predictions about the dangerousness of juvenile sex offenders or different policy choices on agreed-on facts.

If the critical issue is whether most juvenile sex offenders fit the paradigm operational in juvenile courts rather than that in the Megan's Laws, the clear conclusion of the data discussed in chapter 3 favors the nonspecialized, changeable, and nonsexually dangerous image of juvenile sex offenders in juvenile court. Generalizing from the data concerning the dangers posed by the majority of juvenile sex offenders, then, the arguments for registration and notification can be rejected.

But is it possible that, among the heterogeneous assemblage of sex offenders under the age of eighteen, there are a number of subtypes of offenders with fixed propensities toward sexual violence or sexual predation and high levels of likelihood of future sex crime? All future sexual predators in our society pass through adolescence, so there is no doubt that most of tomorrow's predators are subject to the same processes of maturational development as the rest of American youth. If these future predators were easily located and identified while under eighteen, and if instruments for the prediction of sexual danger were not grossly overpredictive, there would be an empirical foundation for the early identification and registration of special classes of chronic offenders.

But the lesson of chapter 3 is that none of the recidivism rates by adolescents convicted of the major types of juvenile sex offenses—forcible sexual assault and indecent liberties with a child—are sufficient for predicting repeat sexual offending at even a 20 percent probability. Under these circumstances, the value system underlying the registration scheme must accommodate an implicit false positive rate of at least 80 percent (because four-fifths of the presumably dangerous will not in fact re-offend). But the underlying values of the juvenile court would likely be out of step with the policy that imposes extensive harms on those who display that low a re-offense rate. To impose on one-time offenders a permanent identity as a potential sexual predator when more than four out of five will not re-offend would be more than a strain on the official worldview of juvenile courts. Therefore, to the extent that such courts make policies that have implications for registration and notification, they will be reluctant to impose sex-offender identities in cases that are anything other than clear. And the juvenile courts of the United States are rarely if ever presented with clear cases of sexually dangerous juvenile offenders until sexually dangerous conduct is repeated after adjudication.

Resolving Conflicts between Juvenile Justice and Systems for Registration and Notification

The best way to minimize the conflict between the principles of juvenile justice and the requirements of registration and notification programs is the careful design of statutory and administrative provisions that relate to adolescent offenders. When the known facts about juvenile sex offenders are measured against the priority concerns of registration schemes, the interests of both systems can often be served with minimum conflict if care is taken.

One Size Doesn't Fit All

One important principle that must be observed in any rational registration and notification scheme is to use criteria for risk and culpability that
consider the developmental status of the offenders. In quantifying the seriousness of sex-offending behavior, to assign ten-year-old J.G. extra points
because his victim was under thirteen, just as one would when quantifying the behavior of an adult offender, is nothing short of bizarre—the
pedophile and the playmate are regarded as equally culpable and equally
dangerous.

Whether the subject is the offender's culpability, the presence of psychological abnormality, future dangerousness, or degree of predation, a
risk assessment scheme that cannot distinguish between the behaviors of
children and youths, on the one hand, and that of adults, on the other,
falls well below the minimum standards that should be expected before
statutes are enacted granting states such potentially destructive power. In a
case like J.G.'s, it could be argued that the one-size-fits-all age classification
of increased dangerousness should have been held a violation of the due
process clause.

As a practical step in avoiding that type of mistake, professional and
political leaders should require separate and specific legislative analysis and
administrative rulemaking for children and youth. And this should require
much more than Idaho's creation of its juvenile sex-offender findings by
adding the word "juvenile" to the legislative findings concerning adult offenders. Youth-specific factual findings and youth-specific policy analysis
should be the only appropriate foundations of rules for judging and classifying the sexual behavior of children and adolescents. And any offenses
such as "lewd conduct" that prohibit consensual contact with young children should never be the basis for community registration if the offender
is within five years of the victim's age.

Options for Registration

One simple legislative approach to ensure that the distinction between juvenile and adult sex offending is not covered up is to exclude all behavior
adjudicated in juvenile courts from registration and notification requirements. Even this broad an exclusion could be designed to provide important information about adolescent sexual behavior for registration systems
if two provisions were added to the basic exclusion. One would make at

least the registration requirements of Megan's Laws applicable if sex offenders have been transferred to criminal courts. This provision is perhaps best restricted to offenders over age sixteen at the time of the offense and to judicial waiver rather than overbroad legislative exclusions from juvenile court jurisdictions (see Feld, 2000). But requiring transfer would help ensure that the case was regarded as serious while protecting more than 95 percent of juvenile sex offenders.

But wouldn't an exemption for juvenile adjudications keep valuable information out of the registration system for juvenile offenders who later become adult threats? Not necessarily. One good approach to information sharing in sex cases might involve conditional record sealing. Once any individual has been convicted of a sex felony as an adult (or within eight years of reaching the age of majority), any juvenile adjudications that involved sex offending would be available to the registration and classification system for the purposes of risk classification, and to provide some data of limited value on an offender's targets and mode of operation. This conditional sealing strategy would exclude any record of sex offending for the great majority of juvenile offenders, and also spare law enforcement authorities a flood of low-risk registrants. Yet the full career details of those who have demonstrated risk in adulthood would be in the system once risk has been confirmed with a registration offense conviction in criminal court. The number of career sex offenders who would be able to hide official records behind the protective policies of juvenile justice would fast approach zero. The number of low-risk juveniles kept from permanent stigma would be quite large.

A variation on the total exclusion strategy is to provide for a special certification hearing before a juvenile court judge in cases of serious sex crime where the juvenile court retains jurisdiction, but to require that the prosecution establish empirically verified indications of sexual danger before registration is required. An adversarial hearing in juvenile court in which the prosecutor bears the burden of proof might lead to a juvenile court finding that could push a youth onto a registration scheme without creating a transfer. Given the present data on juvenile sex offenders, such a proceeding would probably be restricted to multiple recidivists with offenses that were not life threatening or horribly predatory, or very serious offenders still in early or middle teens and thus believed to be too young for transfer. The advantage of having a nontransfer entry to police registration is that it might reduce the use of transfer that was motivated solely to effect registrations. The disadvantage is that it would encourage more recourse to registration in marginal cases.

Community Notification

As with registration, a distinction can be made in community notification systems between providing juvenile court information about offenders who later qualify for notification because of adult offenses (a practice that can be justified) and simply making juvenile behavior itself the basis for community notification (a dangerous and unnecessary step). While a case can be made that some juvenile court adjudications might be the basis for registration with police, the additional requirement of community notification should never be a consequence of a juvenile court finding. Community notification amounts to being branded for life as a sexual offender. It may be difficult to undo the harms generated by sex-offender registration but it is impossible to undo the harms of community notification.

The accommodations and devices discussed above illustrate the variety of options available to legislators and other policymakers who seek to harmonize the need for information about sex offenders and the interests in protecting youthful offenders wherever possible. But the point to be made here is that the various strategies are available only when the focus is on the specific features of juvenile sex offending.

Policy Choice in True Conflicts

The legislative options discussed in the previous section are methods for designing registration systems to avoid a direct clash with the objectives and priorities of juvenile courts in typical juvenile sex cases. It is always preferable to resolve potential conflicts by tailoring legislative rules in such a way that both the interests of juvenile justice and the information needs of registration are properly accommodated. What is necessary to achieve this type of compromise programming is a legislative effort devoted solely to registration in juvenile cases that jointly involves interest groups representing juvenile courts, juvenile offenders, law enforcement, and other actors with direct stakes in the practical operation of a registration system.

Now that the states have accumulated some years of experience with sex-offender registration and notification, perhaps the time is ripe for a renewed effort at rationalizing this aspect of juvenile sex-offender law and policy. But the inertia of state legislatures is notorious, and reform of sex-offender statutes mixes some political risk to policymakers with no real pecuniary incentive. The rules that propelled young J.G.'s status under New Jersey's Megan's Law into that state's highest court may have been silly, but they were not expensive. Under such circumstances, it is more than a little difficult to generate enough pressure so that the reform of existing registration laws becomes a legislative priority. In the short run at least, we can anticipate some of the conflict between juvenile court priorities and the operation of registration provisions in many state systems to persist.

How should such conflicts be resolved? It is clear that juvenile courts usually have the power to protect juveniles who face sex charges from being forced into the registration systems, because a necessary condition for the duty to register is an adjudication that establishes the offender's guilt of a sex charge. For this reason, the adjudication of guilt for charges that are not a predicate for registration or the diversion of cases so that no final disposition is on a juvenile's record would avoid the registration system.

While the capacity to avoid registration in this way is clear, substantial questions remain about whether that sort of procedural sidestepping is appropriate for juvenile courts, as do concerns about compromises in the value of juvenile court records that must be considered.

There is ample precedent in the history and current practice of juvenile courts for manipulating procedural categories in order to serve the interests of accused delinquents. Indeed, it has been argued that the entire delinquency docket of the juvenile court should be regarded as a diversion program from criminal courts (Zimring, 2002). Further, only about half of all arrests and complaints referred to U.S. juvenile courts ever become formal petitions alleging delinquency. The rest are diverted at intake screening by a probation officer's judgment that formal charges are not necessary (Rosenheim, 2002). Even when petitions are filed, the juvenile courts often have more formal "diversion programs" that suspend the proceedings while the youth participates in a supervision or treatment program. The goal of this kind of diversion is to secure the benefits of supervision of the young offender while relieving him of the stigma that comes with being labeled a delinquent.

The way in which a diversionary program can circumvent the registration requirement is illustrated by the facts of the case involving J.G., the ten-year-old boy whose adventures in New Jersey were discussed in chapter 1. The case was never tried in juvenile court, but instead was resolved by a plea of guilty in exchange for an agreement that J.G. would only have to participate in family growth counseling. To avoid the registration consequences, the agreement might have suspended J.G.'s delinquency petition while he completed his counseling program. Successful completion would then result in dismissal of changes. The net effect of this type of policy for those arrested for the first time on juvenile sex charges without extensive violence would be to avoid registration in the 90 percent or so of cases without sex-charge recidivism. For all cases where the extent of punishment and treatment available in diversion did not fall well below the minimum required by the juvenile court's sense of proportional punishment, the outcome would suit the purposes of the court.

Routine diversion to avoid registration and notification would produce some degree of friction with the interests of juvenile court prosecutors, and also result in a loss of valuable information for that narrow band of cases in which such information is helpful to criminal courts and investigative agencies. Prosecutors like guilty pleas and guilty verdicts for a variety of reasons, including the fact that official guilt is a common method of score keeping to measure prosecutorial success. That is why, in cases like J.G.'s, an acknowledgment of guilt is important to a prosecutor even if she is not concerned with later registration. So a judicial diversion policy might displease prosecutors even if judges like it. Some conflict can then be expected on the desirability of a diversion strategy even if the other controls on defendants are the same as in plea cases. But pride in the symbols of prosecutorial success is not as important as avoiding clear harm to the majority of sex delinquents, which should be the most important factor in designing policy.

But what about the loss of potentially valuable information concerning the juvenile careers of persons who then turn out to commit sex offenses as adults? The information loss from the diversion program for first offenders will probably be slight. All juvenile offenders who recidivate while in juvenile court will be in the record system as sex offenders. And information about all those juvenile offenders who do *not* recidivate either as juveniles or adults will not be of value to the stated purposes of a registration/notification system. It is only the offenders who do not re-offend as juveniles but who are later arrested as adults who will not be fully documented in the registration system because of first-time offender juvenile diversion programs. Nobody knows how large this group might be—we do not even know how many adult sex offenders are arrested as juveniles, let alone how many are only arrested one time as juveniles but subsequently identified as adult offenders.

If lawmakers and prosecutors think diversion results in significant information loss, then legislative drafting of a conditional sealing result can obtain the same protection for first-time offenders without compromising the availability of juvenile information for identified adult offenders. Perhaps unhappiness with a diversion program could provide the incentive for prosecutors to press for legislative compromises in cases where overbroad registration systems for juveniles lead to a diversion program response. And if prosecutors desire legislative reforms of this kind, the chances of legislative success are much higher than if prosecutors are indifferent.

Juvenile courts also have the capacity to shield delinquents from sex-offender registration by conviction for nonsex offenses like assault, but this strategy is less well established in the policy history of the juvenile court than diversion, and also needlessly distorts the content of juvenile records. Diversion to avoid stigma is as old as the juvenile court (Zimring, 2002), but relabeling offenses of conviction has no such pedigree. Relabeling also shields the actual first-offense content of all sex offenders from later scrutiny, even if the juvenile re-offends as both a juvenile and adult. Once the system has turned a sex-assault charge into a simple assault conviction, the record cannot be rehabilitated. An effective diversion program that notes a first arrest but does not require registration would remove the need to distort the content of first sex offenses to avoid the gratuitous harm of registration and notification.

Diversion and relabeling were both opposed by the 1993 Task Force report by the National Adolescent Perpetrator Network discussed in chapter 4, which instead expressed faith in the therapeutic value of prosecution and conviction for juvenile sex offenders. But there are three reasons why this objection should not be given much weight. First, when diversion programs send youth into treatment, the Task Force on offender treatment is getting the outcome it most desires. Prosecution and conviction records should be small beer by comparison to this larger priority. Second, the 1993 Task Force did not have registration and notification in mind when it made its recommendations. The report was written before Megan's laws were in place. For all we know, the Task Force might now prefer diversion programs to the harms and dangers of full-scale stigmatization under Megan's Laws. The third reason to discount the preference for adjudication in the 1993 report is that its benefits were supported only by speculation. No follow-up of diverted versus adjudicated sex offenders was cited, and no explicit behavioral theory was developed or found in the literature on human behavior or on criminal justice.

There are, then, three possible approaches to resolving conflicts between the youth protective interests of juvenile justice and the registration and notification schemes that reach back into the juvenile court. The first and best approach is to carefully restructure the legislation governing registration and notification to protect youth while preserving information from juvenile records that concerns persons who later offend as adults. The second is to divert first-time juvenile sex offenders, thereby avoiding adjudication of those who successfully complete diversion programs. The third and least attractive approach is to convict accused sex offenders of nonsex crimes. The juvenile court has long supported the treatment and discipline of defendants diverted from formal adjudication. This is the natural path for minimizing the harm of registration and notification systems when legislative repairs cannot be made.

So the best solution to resolving conflicts between registration statutes and juvenile court policy preferences is the rational restructuring of information sharing systems through legislation. The second best solution is for the juvenile court to pursue its traditional priorities with its traditional tools.

The wave of Megan's Laws that swept the country in the mid-1990s is a potential disaster for youth welfare and the interests of juvenile justice. The policies of the juvenile courts toward adolescent and child offenders were needlessly swept up in the public reaction to lethal violence by adult recidivists. But some good might yet come from this recent trend. Cases like *In re Registrant J. G.* are more than the *reductio ad absurdum* of a legal system blind to the significance of the different stages of human development. They are a wake-up call to all who are concerned about policy toward youth. By raising the stakes in our treatment of young sex offenders, the recent wave of registration and community notification laws may finally provoke the attention and perspective that are the precondition to rational and humane legal policy.

Appendix A

Statutory Provisions Concerning Indecent Sexual Contact
with Minors (in Fifty U.S. States and the District of Columbia)

Prepared by Shanna Connor

State	Age of child "acted upon"	Age of person "committing the act"	Minimum age gap required between actors (in years)*	Exemptions	Name of offense	Statutory provision
Alabama	12–15	19+			Sexual abuse in the second degree	Ala. Code § 13A-6-67
Alaska	13–15	16+	3		Sexual abuse of a minor in the third degree	Alaska Stat. § 11.41.438
	<13	<16	3		Sexual abuse of a minor in the fourth degree	Alaska Stat. § 11.41.440
Arizona	<15				Molestation of child; sexual abuse	Ariz. Rev. Stat. Ann. §§ 13-1410; § 13-1404
Arkansas	<16	18+			Sexual abuse	Ark. Code Ann. § 12-12-503
California	<14				Lewd or lascivious acts	Cal. Penal Code (West) § 288.1
Colorado	<18				Unlawful sexual contact	Colo. Rev. Stat. §18-3-404
Connecticut	<16				Sexual assault in the fourth degree	Conn. Gen. Stat. § 53a-73a
Delaware	<16				Unlawful sexual contact in the second degree	Del. Code Ann. tit. 11, § 53a-73a
District of Columbia	<18				Sexual offense	D.C. Code Ann. §§ 22-4001; 22-3001(8) & (9)

State	Victim age	Perpetrator age	Age difference	Notes	Offense	Statute
	<16		4		Second degree child sexual abuse	D.C. Code Ann. § 22-3009
Florida	12–15	18+			Lewd or lascivious molestation in the second degree	Fla. Stat.Ann. § 800.04(5)(c)(2)
	12–15	<18			Lewd or lascivious molestation in the third degree	Fla. Stat.Ann. § 800.04(5)(d)
Georgia	<18		5	If acts are consensual between persons of the opposite sex and less than 5 years age difference	Sexual abuse	Ga. Code Ann. § 19-7-5
Hawaii	<14				Sexual assault in the third degree	Haw. Rev. Stat. § 707-732
	14 < 16		5	If actors are legally married	Sexual assault in the third degree	Haw. Rev. Stat. § 707-732
Idaho	<16				Lewd conduct with a minor child	Idaho Code § 18-1508
	<16	18+			Sexual abuse of a minor child	Idaho Code § 18-1506
Illinois	9–16	<17			Criminal sexual abuse	Ill. Rev. Stat. ch. 720, 5/12-15
	13–16		<5		Criminal sexual abuse	Ill. Rev. Stat. ch. 720, 5/12-15

State	Age of child "acted upon"	Age of person "committing the act"	Minimum age gap required between actors (in years)*	Exemptions	Name of offense	Statutory provision
Indiana	14–15	18+			Sexual misconduct with a minor	Ind. Code § 35-42-4-9
Iowa	< 18	18+		If actors are married to each other	Lascivious acts with a child; indecent contact with a child	Iowa Code Ann. §§ 709.8; 709.12
Kansas	14–15			If actors are married to each other	Indecent liberties with a child	Kan. Stat. Ann. § 21-3503
Kentucky	< 14				Sexual abuse in the second degree	Ky. Rev. Stat. Ann. § 510.120
Louisiana	< 17		2		Indecent behavior with juveniles	La. Rev. Stat. Ann. § 14:81
Maine	< 14		3	If actors are married to each other	Unlawful sexual contact	Me. Rev. Stat. Ann. tit. 17-A § 255
Maryland	< 14		4		Sexual offense in the third degree	Md. Code Ann., Crim. Law § 3-307
Massachusetts	< 16				Unnatural and lascivious acts with child under 16	Mass. Gen. L. ch. 272 § 35A
Michigan	13–15		5		Fourth degree criminal sexual conduct	Mich. Comp. Laws § 750.520e
Minnesota	< 13		< 3		Criminal sexual conduct in the fourth degree	Minn. Stat. § 609.345

State	Age			Affirmative defense	Offense	Statute
	13–15		4	Affirmative defense: If actor believes complainant was older than 16	Criminal sexual conduct in the fourth degree	Minn. Stat. § 609.345
Mississippi	< 16	18+			Fondling child	Miss. Code Ann. § 97-5-23
Missouri	< 17				Child molestation in the second degree	Mo. Rev. Stat. § 566.068
Montana	< 14		3		Sexual assault	Mont. Code Ann. § 45-5-502
Nebraska	< 17	18+			Debauching a minor	Neb. Rev. Stat. § 28-805
Nevada	< 14				Lewdness with child under 14 years	Nev. Rev. Stat. § 201.230
New Hampshire	< 13				Aggravated felonious sexual assault	N. H. Rev. Stat. Ann. § 632-A:2(II)
New Jersey	< 13		4		Sexual assault	N.J. Rev. Stat. 2C:14-2(b)
New Mexico	< 13				Criminal sexual contact of a minor in the third degree	N.M. Stat. Ann § 30-9-13

State	Age of child "acted upon"	Age of person "committing the act"	Minimum age gap required between actors (in years)*	Exemptions	Name of offense	Statutory provision
New York	< 14				Sexual abuse in the second degree	N.Y. Penal Law § 130.60
North Carolina	13–15		4+	If actors are married	Sexual offense of person who is 13–15 years old	N.C. Gen. Stat. § 14-27.7A
North Dakota	15–17	18+			Sexual assault	N.D. Cent. Code § 12.1-20-07
Ohio	13–15	18+	4		Sexual imposition	Ohio Rev. Code Ann. § 2907.06(A)(4)
Oklahoma	< 16		3		Lewd or indecent proposals or acts as to a child under 16	Okla. Stat. Ann. tit. 21, § 1123

State	Age			Offense	Notes	Citation
Oregon	<18		3	Sexual abuse in the third degree	Defense: less than a three-year age difference	Or. Rev. Stat. §§ 163.315; 163.345
Pennsylvania	<16		4	Indecent assault	If actors are married to each other	Pa. Cons. Stat. Ann. tit. 18, §§ 3126; 3102
Rhode Island	<15			Second degree child molestation sexual assault		R.I. Gen. Laws § 11-37-8.3
South Carolina	<16	14+		Committing or attempting lewd act upon child under 16		S.C. Code Ann. § 16-15-140
South Dakota	<16	<16		Sexual contact with child under 16 years of age	If actors are married	S.D. Codified Laws Ann. § 22-22-7.3
Tennessee	<13			Aggravated sexual battery		Tenn. Code Ann. § 39-13-504
Texas	<17		3	Indecency with a child	Affirmative defense: actor was less than 3 years older and of the opposite sex and did not use force or duress against the victim	Tex. Penal Code Ann. § 21.11
Utah	<14			Sexual abuse of a child		Utah Code Ann. § 76-5-404.1
Utah	14–15		7	Sexual abuse of a minor		Utah Code Ann. § 76-5-401.1

State	Age of child "acted upon"	Age of person "committing the act"	Minimum age gap required between actors (in years)*	Exemptions	Name of offense	Statutory provision
	16–17		10		Unlawful sexual conduct with a 16 or 17 year old	Utah Code Ann. § 76-5-401.2
Vermont	< 16				Lewd or lascivious conduct with child	Vt. Stat. Ann. tit. 13, § 2602
Virginia	< 14	18+			Taking indecent liberties with children	Va. Code Ann. § 18.2-370
	< 14	13–17	5		Indecent liberties by children**	Va. Code Ann. § 18.2-370.01
Washington	14–15	18+	4	If actors are married to each other	Child molestation in the third degree	Wash. Rev. Code § 9A.44.089
	16–17	18+	5	If actors are married to each other	Sexual misconduct with a minor in the second degree	Wash. Rev. Code § 9A.44.096
West Virginia	< 16		4	Defense: if defendant is less than 16 or if defendant was less than 4 years older	Sexual abuse in the third degree	W.Va. Code § 61-8B-9
Wisconsin	< 16				Second degree sexual assault of a child	Wis. Stat. Ann. § 948.02(2)

| Wyoming | < 14 | 18+ | | Sexual assault in the third degree | Wyo. Stat. § 6-2-304 |
| | < 16 | 4 | Affirmative defense: If actor reasonably believed complainant was 16 years old or older | Sexual assault in the third degree | Wyo. Stat. § 6-2-304 |

---

* Where an age gap is written into a state statute, it requires that the person "committing the act" must be older than the person being "acted upon" by the number of years outlined.

** This statute defines indecent liberties as "knowingly and intentionally" exposing ones sexual or genital parts to another.

Appendix B

Topics in Sex-Offender Treatment

The 1993 Task Force report (National Adolescent Perpetrator Network, 1993) describes the thirty-four items listed below as a "partial list" of issues that treatment of sex offenders should address (p. 48). In this appendix, I organize the issues into three categories, reflecting my judgment about whether they represent matters that all adolescents need to address, matters of special concern for adolescents with significant histories of juvenile offending, or issues that are of special concern of juvenile sex offenders only. But I provide the list of topics so that readers will be free to make their own classification of issues into categories.

The majority of issues identified as important in sex-offender treatment are standard concerns for all youth; this is true of twenty-three of the thirty-four topics below. Another six of the thirty-four topics seem to me to be of special importance to young persons with significant histories of criminal offending of any kind—issues like accountability for exploitive behavior, impulsivity, and empathy for victims. The robber and burglar have just as much need for victim empathy and impulse control as most teen sex offenders. Only five of the listed issues seem to be limited to sex offenders only, and two of those topics—dealing with deviant fantasizing and long-term management of sexually deviant impulses—are only appropriate for the unknown proportion of juvenile sex offenders who are at risk for sexual deviance.

The fact that 80 percent of the topics covered by juvenile sex-offender treatment are relevant to the needs of much broader sectors of the youth population does not mean that most of the programs now administered spend 80 percent of treatment time on issues applicable to all teens. Attempts to monitor, control, punish, and disclose sexual offending receive the lion's share of emphasis in the Task Force report. It is safe to assume they also get much more attention in therapy sessions for sex offenders.

Topics in Sex-Offender Treatment by Type of Concern Reflected

ISSUES FOR ALL ADOLESCENTS

- Denial, minimization, and projecting blame
- Thinking errors/irrational thinking
- Self-responsibility in sexual and nonsexual functioning
- Power and control behaviors/covert exploitation
- History of client's own victimization
- Life history/autobiography
- Helplessness and lack of control
- Delusions of persecution
- Anger management and frustration tolerance
- Feeling identification and management
- Substance abuse/addictive behaviors
- Self-esteem and identity
- Positive sexual development/identity
- Sex education/sexually transmitted disease including AIDS
- Sex-role stereotyping
- Cultural influences
- Sexual identity issues; homosexuality/homophobia
- Communication/social skills training
- Assertiveness training
- Dating/relationship building
- Employment/vocational issues
- Family dysfunction and sibling issues
- Educational issues

ISSUES OF SPECIAL CONCERN FOR DELINQUENTS

- Accountability for all abusive or exploitative behaviors
- Apparently irrelevant or unrelated decisions that set up a high risk situation
- Irresponsible decision making/high-risk behaviors
- Empathy development/victim personalization

- Impulsivity and poor judgment
- Values clarification, including victim empathy

ISSUES OF SPECIAL CONCERN FOR SEX OFFENDERS

- Contributing factors to cycle of abusive behavior
- History of offending behavior
- Long-term management of sexually deviant impulses
- Ability to experience pleasure in nonexploitive activities
- Arousal patterns/deviant fantasizing

Sources: Topics for Therapy: Assumption 186, National Adolescent Perpetrator Network, 1993; classification by author.

Appendix C

Juvenile Sex-Offender Recidivism

Prepared by Chrysanthi Leon

For my analysis in this book, I divide the recidivism studies as falling under one of three categories: justice system, correctional, or clinical. A justice system sample is a cross section or population of all juvenile offenders coming to the attention of the courts on sex charges. It is the most representative study for policy analysis. A correctional population or sample is all or a cross section of sex offenders confined in a penal facility. It is much less representative of the total population of adolescent sexual offenders. A clinical population comprises offenders or others in treatment at a particular place or group of places. It is the least representative sample of the juvenile offender population. In addition, there are many combinations of these three sampling strategies, including all published meta-analyses.

This appendix reproduces the results of both unpublished and published justice system studies and the results of a less comprehensive group of recent clinical and correctional samples.

Unpublished Justice System Studies

Gfellner, B. M. (2000). *Profiling adolescent sex offenders: Offending history, personal characteristics, treatment and recidivism.* Research report, Sex Offender Treatment Advisory Group (SOTAG). Brandon, Manitoba. Available at www.gfellner@brandonu.ca.

Sample:	75 male adolescent sexual offenders from probation files
Follow-up:	Up to 4.25 years (no mean given)
Measure:	Criminal charges
Overall recidivism:	2.7% (2)
Sex offenders (27)	
Sex offenses:	3.7% (1)
Nonsex offenses:	14.8% (4)
Offenders who committed sex and nonsex offenses (48)	
Sex offenses:	2.1% (1)
Nonsex offenses:	31.3% (15)
Nonsex offenders (29)	
Sex offenses:	0
"Nonsex offenses:	21.4% (listed as 6/28)

National Council on Crime and Delinquency (NCCD), prepared by Richard G. Wiebush. (1996). *Juvenile sex offenders: Characteristics, system response, and recidivism.* Final Report. Available from the National Criminal Justice Reference Service, 800–851-3420. A cross-site empirical portrait of court-involved juvenile sex offenders (including hands-off offenses); results listed here for (1) Baltimore, MD, (2) Lucas County, OH, and (3) San Francisco, CA.

Follow-up:	18 months, plus extended follow-ups up to 35 months
Measure:	Arrests
Overall Sexual Recidivism:	3.2%–5.5%

1. Baltimore, MD (213): Youths residing in Baltimore in fiscal year 1992 who were charged with sex offenses.

Recidivism, 18 months	
Sex offenses:	3.3%
Nonsex offenses:	43.6%
Violent offenses:	14.1%
Extended	
Sex offenses:	4.2%
Nonsex offenses:	50.7%
Violent offenses:	19.7%

2. Lucas County, OH (188): Split sample: referral cohort considered all county residents referred to juvenile court for sex offenses 1/92–9/92 (62) and the adjudicated JSO cohort consisted of all youth in the referral cohort and an additional

116 adjudicated JSOs from 1990 and 1991.

Referral Cohort (62)

Recidivism, 18 months

Sex offenses:	3.2%
Nonsex offenses:	21.0%
Violent offenses:	1.6%

Extended

Sex offenses:	3.2%
Nonsex offenses:	30.7%
Violent offenses:	1.6%

3. San Francisco, CA (91): All youths residing in San Francisco who were charged with sex offenses between 1/90–9/92.

Recidivism, 18 months

Sex offenses:	5.5%
Nonsex offenses:	35.1%
Violent offenses:	19.8%

Extended

Sex offenses:	5.5%
Nonsex offenses:	42.9%
Violent offenses:	30.8%

Published Justice System Studies

Doshay, L. J. (1943). *The boy sex offender and his later career.* New York: Grune & Stratton.

Sample:	256 (108 sex-only offenders and 148 general delinquents with a reported sex offense)
Follow-up:	About 4 years minimum
Measure:	Criminal conviction when 16 or over and juvenile recidivism (under 16)
Recidivism:	None of the sex-only offenders re-offended. 3.1 % (8) of the general delinquents had a "sex failure" (8 delinquents committed 10 offenses /"sex violations" or 3.9%)
Any re-offending:	16.8% (43)

Lab, S. P., Shields, G., & Schondel, C. (1993). Research note: An evaluation of juvenile sexual offender treatment. *Crime and Delinquency, 39,* 543–553. Retrospective evaluation of juvenile court files.

Sample: 155 youth referred to court-based sex-offender treatment program between 1/2/88–4/30/91, 46 assigned to sex-specific treatment and 109 assigned to non-sex-specific interventions (not random assignments).

Follow-up: 1–3 years
Measure: Arrests
Treated (46)
  Sex offenses: 2.2% (1)
  Any offense: 24% (11)
Comparison (109)
  Sex offenses: 3.7% (4)
  Any offense: 17% (18)

Rasmussen, L. A. (1999). Factors related to recidivism among juvenile sexual offenders. *Sexual Abuse: A Journal of Research and Treatment, 11*(1), 69–85. This retrospective study examined juvenile court case records of first-time juvenile sex offenders, excluding noncoercive offenses.

Sample: 170
Follow-up: 5 years or until 19th birthday
Measure: Conviction
Sex offenses: 14.1% (24)
Nonsex offenses: 54.1% (91)
Any offense: 58.8% (100)

Correctional Studies

Hagan, M. P., Gust-Brey, K. L., Cho, M. E., & Dow, E. (2001). Eight-year comparative analyses of adolescent rapists, adolescent child molesters, other adolescent delinquents and the general population. *International Journal of Offender Therapy and Comparative Criminology, 45*(3), 314–324.

Sample: 150 male juveniles aged 12–19 detained at a secure juvenile correctional facility in Wisconsin.

Follow-up: 8 years
Measure: Conviction
Sex-offense Recidivism
  Sex offenders (100):   18% (18)
    child sexual offenders (50):   20% (10)
    adolescent rapists (50):   16% (8)
  Nonsex offenders (50):   10% (5)

Långström, N. (2002). Long-term follow-up of criminal recidivism in young offenders: Temporal patterns and risk factors. *Psychology, Crime & Law, 8,* 41–58.

Sample:	117 young sex offenders (15–20) subjected to pre-sentence forensic evaluation in Sweden from 1980–1995 (includes noncontact offenders).
Follow-up:	Mean 115 months (9.58 years)
Measure:	Conviction
Sex offenses:	30%
Violent, nonsexual:	42%

Leidecke, D., & Marbibi, M. (2000). *Risk assessment and recidivism in juvenile sexual offenders: A validation study of the Static-99.* Austin, TX: Texas Youth Commission. Available from 4900 N. Lamar Blvd., P.O. Box 4260, Austin, TX 78765.

Sample:	72 juvenile sex offenders
Follow-up:	3 years
Measure:	Arrests
Recidivism	
Sex offenses:	3/72

Milloy, C. D. (1994). *A comparative study of juvenile sex offenders and Nonsex Offenders.* Washington State Institute for Public Policy. Available at www.wa.gov/wsipp/pubs.html.

Sample:	265 male convicted juvenile offenders serving sentences in Division of Juvenile Rehabilitation facilities on 2/14/90. 59 juvenile sex offenders (including noncontact offenses) and 206 nonsex offenders.
Follow-up:	3 years
Measure:	Conviction
Sex Offenders (59)	
Sex offenses:	0
Violent offense:	18.6% (11)
Nonviolent offenses:	37.3% (22)
Any offense:	44.1% (26)
Nonsex offenders (206)	
Sex offenses:	0.5% (1)
Violent offenses:	21.3% (42)
Nonviolent offenses:	54.8% (108)
Any offense:	58.4% (115)

Miner, M. H. (2002). Factors associated with recidivism in juveniles: An analysis of serious juvenile sex offenders. *Journal of Research in Crime and Delinquency, 39*(4): 421–436.

Sample:	86 of 121 residents of corrections-based juvenile sex-offender program in Minnesota, ages 14–19, including noncontact offenders, admitted between 3/10/93–12/27/95.
Follow-up:	Mean time at risk 4.29 years
Measure:	Arrest, conviction, or parole violation for a new crime
Recidivism	
Sex offenses:	8% (7)
Any offense:	55% (47)

Clinical Studies

Becker, J. V. (1990). Treating adolescent sexual offenders. *Professional Psychology: Research and Practice, 21*, 362–365.

Sample:	Of 300 adolescent sexual offenders who were evaluated, 205 entered treatment and 52 both completed treatment and were available for interview.
Follow-up:	1 year
Measure:	Referrals and self-reports of sexual crimes
Sexual recidivism:	5/52

Borduin, C. M., Henggeler, S. W., Blaske, D. M., & Stein, R. J. (1990). Multisystemic treatment of adolescent sexual offenders. *International Journal of Offender Therapy and Comparative Criminology, 34*, 105–113.

Sample:	16 adolescent sex offenders (including exhibitionism) in outpatient treatment.
Follow-up:	Mean 3 years
Measure:	Arrest
Recidivism	
MST treated	
Sex offenses:	12.5%
Nonsex offenses:	25%
Individually treated	
Sex offenses:	75%
Nonsex offenses:	50%

Cooper, H. (2000). *Long-term follow-up of a community-based treatment program for adolescent sex offenders*. Unpublished master's thesis, Lakehead University, Thunder Bay, Ontario.

Sample:	89 adolescent sexual offenders in treatment
Follow-up:	Mean 7 years
Measure:	Criminal conviction

Recidivism

10 months treatment (41)

Sex offenses:	2.4% (1)
Nonsex offenses:	29.3% (12)
Serious offenses:	17.1% (7)

Incomplete treatment (23)

Sex offenses:	17.4% (4)
Nonsex offenses:	60.9% (14)
Serious offenses:	56.5% (13.5)

Assessment only (25)

Sex offenses:	4.0% (1)
Nonsex offenses:	44.0% (11)
Serious offenses:	36.0% (9)

Kahn, T. J., & Chambers, H. A. (1991). Assessing reoffense risk with juvenile sexual offenders. *Child Welfare, 70*(3), 333–345.

Sample:	221 juvenile sexual offenders who enter treatment programs in Washington State.
Follow-up:	Mean 20.4 months
Measure:	Juvenile court records showing criminal convictions

Recidivism

Sex offenses:	7.5%
Violent offenses:	6.6%
Any offense:	44.8%

McConaghy, N., Blaszczynski, A. Armstrong, M. S., & Kidson, W. (1989). Resistance to treatment of adolescent sex offenders. *Archives of Sexual Behaviour, 18*, 97–107.

Sample:	6 adolescent sexual offenders, ages 14–19, including noncontact offenders, referred for treatment.
Measure:	Detected re-offenses (not charges or convictions)
Sexual Recidivism:	3/6

Prentky, R., Harris, B., Frizzell, K., & Righthand, S. (2000). An actuarial procedure for assessing risk with juvenile sex offenders. *Sexual Abuse: A Journal of Research and Treatment, 12,* 71–93.

Sample:	96 juvenile sex offenders referred for treatment in Philadelphia (2/3 adjudicated, 1/3 nonadjudicated), including hands-off offenses.
Follow-up:	1 year
Measure:	Court record, self & parent report
Sex offenses:	3%
Any offense:	11%

Rubinstein, M., Yeager, C. A., Goodstein, C., & Lewis, D. O. (1993). Sexually assaultive male juveniles: A follow-up. *American Journal of Psychiatry, 150,* 262–265.

Sample:	19 violent male juvenile sexual offenders (excluding noncontact offenders) and 58 male violent juveniles incarcerated in Connecticut.
Follow-up:	8 years
Measure:	Arrest and incarceration
Recidivism	
Sex Offenders (19)	
Sex offenses:	37% (7)
Nonsexual violent offenses:	89% (17)
Nonsex Offenders (58)	
Sex offenses:	10% (6)
Nonsexual violent offenses:	69% (40)

Schram, D. D., Milloy, C. D., & Rowe, W. E. (1991). *Juvenile sex offenders: A follow-up study of reoffense behavior.* Olympia, WA: Washington State Institute for Public Policy. Available at www.wa.gov/wsipp/pubs.html.

Sample:	197 male juvenile sex offenders, included noncontact offenders, aged 8–18 years who participated in offense-specific treatment at 10 project sites in 1984.
Follow-up:	2–7 years
Measure:	Arrests and convictions
Arrests	
Sex offenses:	12.2% (24)
Any offense:	62.9% (124)
Violent felony:	15.2% (30)

Nonviolent felony:	40% (78)
Misdemeanor:	52.8% (104)
Convictions	
Sex offenses:	10.2% (20)
Any offense:	57.9% (114)
Violent felony:	9.1% (18)
Nonviolent felony:	36.5% (72)
Misdemeanor:	43.7% (86)

Meta-Analyses

Alexander, M. A. 1999. Sexual offender treatment efficacy revisited. *Sexual Abuse: A Journal of Research and Treatment, 11*(2), 101–116. Meta-analysis of 79 sexual-offender treatment outcome studies, including 10,988 subjects. Studies that included female and developmentally disabled offenders or that included fewer than 10 subjects were excluded from the analysis. In addition, the analysis excluded subjects who did not complete treatment. Recidivism was measured, when possible, as arrest for a new sex offense. The analysis included 1,025 juvenile subjects, with a recidivism rate of 7.1% (73).

Caldwell, M. F. (2002). What we do not know about juvenile sexual reoffense risk. *Child Maltreatment, 7*(4): 291–302. This article gives an overview of recidivism studies of juveniles sexual offenders. By analyzing 25 studies that varied across several dimensions, the researcher finds that juvenile sex offenders are on average six times more likely to be arrested for nonsex offenses than sex offenses. Sex offenses accounted for an average of 24.6% of recidivism.

References

Abel, G. G., Mittelman M. S., & Becker, J. (1985). Sexual offenders: Results of assessment and recommendations for treatment. In C. D. Webster, M. H. Ben-Aron & S. J. Hucker (Eds.), *Clinical criminology: the assessment and treatment of criminal behaviour.* Toronto: M & M Graphics.

Alexander, M. A. (1999). Sexual offender treatment efficacy revisited. *Sexual Abuse: A Journal of Research and Treatment, 11*(2), 101–116.

Allen, F. A. (1964). *The borderland of criminal justice: Essays in law and criminology.* Chicago: University of Chicago Press.

American Psychiatric Association. (2000). *Diagnostic and statistical manual of mental disorders* (4th ed. [1994], text revision). Washington, DC: American Psychiatric Association.

Association for the Treatment of Sexual Abusers. (2000). *The effective legal management of juvenile sexual offenders.* Position statement adopted by the ATSA Executive Board, March 11. Available at www.atsa.com/ppjuvenile.html.

Becker, J. V. (1998). What we know about the characteristics and treatment of adolescents who have committed sexual offenses. *Child Maltreatment, 3*(4), 317–329.

Bertillon, A. (1889). *Alphonse Bertillon's instructions for taking descriptions of the identification of criminals, and others, by the means of anthropometric indications.* Chicago: American Bertillon Prison Bureau.

Blumstein, A., Cohen, J., Roth, J., & Visher, A. (Eds.). (1986). *Criminal careers and "career criminals."* Report of the National Academy of Sciences Panel on Research on Criminal Careers. Washington, DC: National Academy Press.

Boirduin, C. M., Henggeler, S. W., Blasker, D. M., & Stein, J. (1990). Multisystemic treatment of adolescent sex offenders. *International Journal of Offender Therapy and Comparative Criminology, 34,* 105–113.

Bremer, J. F. (1992). Serious juvenile sex offenders: Treatment and long-term follow-up. *Psychiatric Annals, 22,* 326–332.

Burton, D. L., & Smith-Darden, J. P. (2000). *1996 nationwide survey. A survey of treatment programs & models serving children with sexual behavior problems, adolescent sex offenders, and adult sex offenders. A summary of the past ten years of specialized treatment with projections for the coming decade.* Brandon, Manitoba: Safer Society Press.

Burton, D. L., & Smith-Darden, J. P. (2001). *North American survey of sexual abuser treatment and models summary data 2000.* Brandon, Manitoba: Safer Society Press.

Caldwell, M. F. (2002). What we do not know about juvenile sexual reoffense risk. *Child Maltreatment, 7*(4), 291–302.

Colorado Department of Public Safety. 2000 (January). *Elements of change: Highlighting trends and issues in the criminal justice system.* Office of Research and Statistics, Division of Criminal Justice. Available online at www.dcj.state.co.us/ors/pdf/docs/eoc51.pdf.

Currie, B. (1963). *Selected essays on the conflict of laws.* Durham: Duke University Press.

Dawson, R. (1992). An empirical study of *Kent* style juvenile transfers to criminal court. *St. Mary's Law Journal, 23,* 975.

Doak, J. E. (2002). Modern juvenile justice in Europe. In M. K. Rosenheim, F. E. Zimring, D. S. Tanenhaus & B. Dohrn (Eds.), *A century of juvenile justice.* Chicago: University of Chicago Press.

Doshay, L. J. (1943). *The boy sex offender and his later career.* New York: Grune & Stratton.

Eberle, P. (1993). *The abuse of innocence: The McMartin Preschool trial.* Amherst, MA: Prometheus Press.

Elliot, D. (1994). Serious violent offenders: Onset, developmental course, and termination. *Criminology, 32,* 1.

Elstein, S. G., & Davis, Noy. (1997). *Sexual relationships between adult males and young teen girls: Exploring the legal and social responses.* Washington, DC: American Bar Association, Center on Children and the Law.

Fagan, J., & Zimring, F. E. (2000). *The changing borders of juvenile justice: Transfer of adolescents to the criminal court.* Chicago: University of Chicago Press.

Feld, B. C. (1999). *Bad kids: Race and the transformation of the juvenile court.* New York: Oxford University Press.

Feld, B. C. (2000). *Cases and materials on juvenile justice administration.* St. Paul: West Group.

Flexner, B., & Baldwin, R. N. (1916). *Juvenile courts and probation.* New York: Century Co.

Garfinkle, E. (2003). Coming of age in America: The misapplication of sex-offender registration and community notification laws to juveniles. *California Law Review, 93,* 163–208.

Gfellner, B. M. (2000). *Profiling adolescent sex offenders: Offending history, personal characteristics, treatment and recidivism (research report).* Brandon, Manitoba: Sex Offender Treatment Advisory Group.

Greenwood, P. W., & Turner, S. (1987). *Selective incapacitation revisited: Why the high-rate offenders are hard to predict.* Santa Monica: RAND.

Groth, A. N., Longo, R. E., & McFadin, J. B. (1982). Undetected recidivism among rapists and child molesters. *Crime and Delinquency, 128,* 450–458.

Harling, M. (1996). *Origins of the New York State Bureau of Identification.* New York: New York State Division of Criminal Justice Services.

Hawkins, G., & Zimring, F. E. (1989). *Pornography in a free society.* New York: Cambridge University Press.

Hoover, J. E. (1947, March). "How safe is your daughter?" *American Magazine.*

Hoover, J. E. (1955, March). "How safe is your youngster?" *American Magazine.*

Hunter, J. A., & Lexier, L. J. (1998). Ethical and legal issues in the assessment and treatment of juvenile sex offenders. *Child Maltreatment, 3*(4), 339–348.

Institute of Judicial Administration, American Bar Association. (1977). *I.J.A.-A.B.A. Standards 1977.* Juvenile Justice Standards Project. Chicago: American Bar Association.

Kinsey, A. C., Pomeroy, W. B., & Martin, C. E. (1948). *Sexual behavior in the human male.* Philadelphia: W. B. Saunders.

Lab, S. P., Shields, G., & Schondel, C. (1993). Research note: An evaluation of juvenile sexual offender treatment. *Crime and Delinquency, 39,* 543–553.

Laub, J. H. (2002). A century of delinquency research and delinquency theory. In M. K. Rosenheim, F. E. Zimring, D. S. Tanenhaus & B. Dohrn (Eds.), *A century of juvenile justice.* Chicago: University of Chicago Press.

Leidecke, D., & Marbibi, M. (2000). *Risk assessment and recidivism in juvenile sexual offenders: A validation study of the Static-99.* Austin, TX: Texas Youth Commission.

Lynch, J. (1999). *Survey measurement of violence against women and related topics.* Handouts for presentation at the 1999 National Institute of Justice workshop on Criminal Justice Data: Women and Crime. Available online at www.icpsr.umich.edu/NACJD/SUMMER/NIJ1999/lynch.pdf.

Man, C. D., & Cronan, J. P. (2001–2002). Forecasting sexual abuse in prison: The prison subculture of masculinity as a backdrop for "deliberate indifference." *Journal of Criminal Law and Criminology, 92*, 127–185.

McCurley, C., Sickmund, M., & Snyder, H. N. (2003). Violent juvenile sex offenders. *Juvenile offenders and victims: National report series bulletin.* Washington, DC: Office of Juvenile Justice and Delinquency Prevention.

Milloy, C. D. (1994). *A comparative study of juvenile sex offenders and non-sex offenders.* Olympia, WA: Washington State Institute for Public Policy.

Moffitt, T. (1993). Life-course persistent and adolescent-limited antisocial behavior: A developmental taxonomy. *Psychological Review, 100*, 674–701.

Morris, N. (1974). *The future of imprisonment.* Chicago: University of Chicago Press.

Morris, N., & Tonry, M. H. (1990). *Between prison and probation: Intermediate punishments in a rational sentencing system.* New York: Oxford University Press.

National Adolescent Perpetrator Network. (1993). The revised report from the National Task Force on Juvenile Sexual Offending. *Juvenile and Family Court Journal, 44*(4), 1–115.

National Incident-Based Reporting System (NIBRS) data provided by Harold Snyder, United States Office of Juvenile Justice and Delinquency Prevention, National Center for Juvenile Justice. Pittsburgh, PA.

National Research Council. (2003). *The polygraph and lie detection.* Board on Behavioral, Cognitive, and Sensory Sciences and Education, Committee on National Statistics. Available online at http://www. nap.edu/books/0309084369/html.

Office of the Inspector of Custodial Services. (2003). *Vulnerable and predatory prisoners in Western Australia: A review of policy and practice.* Report No. 15. Perth, Australia: Office of the Inspector of Custodial Services.

Platt, A. (1969). *The child savers: The invention of delinquency.* Chicago: University of Chicago Press.

Righthand, S., & Welch, C. (2001). *Juveniles who have sexually offended: A review of the professional literature.* Washington, DC: Office of Juvenile Justice and Delinquency Prevention.

Rosenheim, M. K. (2002). The modern American juvenile court. In M. K. Rosenheim, F. E. Zimring, D. S. Tanenhaus & B. Dohrn (Eds.), *A century of juvenile justice.* Chicago: University of Chicago Press.

Rosenheim, M. K., Zimring, F. E., Tanenhaus, D. S., & Dohrn, B. (Eds.). *A century of juvenile justice.* Chicago: University of Chicago Press.

Russell, D. E. H. (1982). *Rape in Marriage.* New York: MacMillan.

San Francisco Chronicle. (2000, November 9). "Police Investigating Reported Kidnap-Rape—Middle School Students Arrested in Berkeley."

Schlossman, S. (1977). *Love and the American delinquent: The theory and practice of "progressive" juvenile justice, 1825–1920*. Chicago: University of Chicago Press.

Schram, D. D., Milloy, C. D., & Rowe, W. E. (1991). *Juvenile sex offenders: A follow-up study of reoffense behavior*. Olympia, WA: Washington State Institute for Public Policy.

Sipe, R., Jensen, E. L., & Everett, R. S. (1998). Adolescent sexual offenders grown up: Recidivism in young adulthood. *Criminal Justice and Behavior, 25*, 109–124.

Spaccarelli, S., Bowden, B., Coatsworth, J. D., & Kim, S. (1997). Psychosocial correlates of male sexual aggression in a chronic delinquent sample. *Criminal Justice and Behavior, 24*(1), 71–95.

Tanenhaus, D. S. (2002). The evolution of juvenile courts in the early twentieth century: Beyond the myth of immaculate construction. In M. K. Rosenheim, F. E. Zimring, D. S. Tanenhaus & B. Dohrn (Eds.), *A century of juvenile justice*. Chicago: University of Chicago Press.

Tarvis, C. (2003, February 28). "Mind Games: Psychological Warfare between Therapists and Scientists." *Chronicle of Higher Education*.

Teitelbaum, L. (2002). Status offenses and status offenders. In M. K. Rosenheim, F. E. Zimring, D. S. Tanenhaus & Bernardine Dohrn (Eds.), *A century of juvenile justice*. Chicago: University of Chicago Press.

Trivits, L. C., & Reppucci, N. D. (2002). Application of Megan's Law to juveniles. *American Psychologist, 57*(9), 691–704.

U.S. Department of Commerce, Bureau of the Census. (2000). *Statistical abstract of the United States*. Washington, DC: Government Printing Office.

U.S. Department of Health and Human Services, Administration on Children, Youth and Families. (2003). *Child maltreatment 2001*. Washington, DC: U.S. Government Printing Office.

U.S. Department of Health and Welfare, National Institute of Child Health and Human Development. (2000). *National longitudinal study of adolescent health*. Washington, DC: Government Printing Office.

U.S. Department of Justice, Bureau of Justice Statistics. (2002). *Imprisonment in the United States*. Washington, DC: Government Printing Office.

U.S. Department of Justice, Federal Bureau of Investigation. (1976–1984, 1985–1999, 2000–2001). *Crime in the United States*. Washington, DC: Government Printing Office.

U.S. Department of Justice, Office of the Attorney General. (1999). *Megan's law:*

Final guidelines for the Jacob Wetterling Crimes against Children and Sexually Violent Offender Registration Act, as amended. 64 Fed. Reg. 572, 579.

Wiebush, R. G. (1996). *Juvenile sex offenders: Characteristics, system response, and recidivism. Final report.* Oakland, CA: National Council on Crime and Delinquency.

Wolfgang, M. E., Figlio, R. M., & Sellin, J. T. (1972). *Delinquency in a birth cohort.* Chicago: University of Chicago Press.

Yochelson, S., & Samenow, S. E. (1976). *The criminal personality.* New York : Aronson.

Zimring, F. E. (1978). *Confronting youth crime.* Report of the Twentieth Century Fund Task Force for Young Offenders. New York: Holmes & Meier.

Zimring, F. E. (1982). *The changing legal world of adolescence.* New York: Free Press.

Zimring, F. E. (1998). *American youth violence.* New York: Oxford University Press.

Zimring, F. E. (2000). The punitive necessity of waiver. In J. Fagan & F. E. Zimring (Eds.), *The changing borders of juvenile justice.* Chicago: University of Chicago Press.

Zimring, F. E. (2002). The common thread: Diversion in the jurisprudence of juvenile courts. In M. K. Rosenheim, F. E. Zimring, D. S. Tanenhaus & B. Dohrn (Eds.), *A century of juvenile justice.* Chicago: University of Chicago Press.

Zimring, F. E., Hawkins, G., & Kamin, S. (2001). *Punishment and democracy: Three strikes and you're out in California.* New York: Oxford University Press.

Index

with methods and assumptions of report by, 78–81; proposal of prosecution as treatment by, 91–92; proposals of, compared to other approaches, 93–95; proposals of, contrasted with modern juvenile justice and, 95; proposals of, contrasted with other therapies, 95–97; representativeness of therapists and, 92–93; role of adversarial therapists and, 84–86; taking authority away from legal system by, 92; therapist-patient privilege and, 136; types of treatments proposed by, 89–93; unasked questions of, 86–88

Nebraska, statutory provisions for minors in, 165

Nevada, statutory provisions for minors in, 165

New Hampshire, statutory provisions for minors in, 165

New Jersey: case story of sex offender in, 3–7; Megan's Law in, 4, 5–6; statutory provisions for minors in, 165

New Mexico, statutory provisions for minors in, 165

New York, statutory provisions for minors in, 166

nonpredatory peer sex, policies for, 125–28

nonsex offenses, trends in prisoners incarcerated for, vs. sex offenses, 35

North Carolina, statutory provisions for minors in, 166

North Dakota, statutory provisions for minors in, 166

notification laws, 33; resolving conflicts between juvenile justice and, 152–53. *See also* Megan's Law

offender registration, 32

Office of the Inspector of Custodial Services, 26

Ohio, statutory provisions for minors in, 166

Oklahoma, statutory provisions for minors in, 166

Oregon, statutory provisions for minors in, 167

other sexual assaults, increase in growth rate of, 35, 36f

other sexual offenses, arrests rates for juveniles for, 44f, 45

paraphilia, sexual offenses and, 30

pedophilia, 64–65

peeping Toms, 20

Pennsylvania, statutory provisions for minors in, 167

Platt, A., 94

polygraphs, 137–39

Pomeroy, W. B., 21

pornography, 20; decriminalization of, 32

Prentky, R., 180

privacy, therapist-patient privilege and, 135–36

prosecution, as treatment, 91–92

prostitution, 20

psychopathology, juvenile sex offending and, 64–66

public indecency, 19–20

rape: arrests for, 23–24; forcible, 17; reporting of, 20; statutory,